NAMING OF THE BONES

John F. Deane was born on Achill Island in 1943. He founded *Poetry Ireland* – the National Poetry Society – and *The Poetry Ireland Review* in 1978, and is the founder of The Dedalus Press, of which he was editor from 1985 until 2006. In 2008 he was visiting scholar in the Burns Library of Boston College. He was Teilhard de Chardin Fellow in Christian Studies at Loyola University, Chicago, in 2016 and taught a course in poetry. John F. Deane's poetry has been translated and published in France, Bulgaria, Macedonia, Romania, Italy, Slovakia, Sweden and other countries. His poems in Italian won the 2002 Premio Internazionale di Poesia Città di Marineo. His fiction has been published by Blackstaff Press in Belfast; his most recent novel *Where No Storms Come* was published by Blackstaff in 2011. He is the recipient of the O'Shaughnessy Award for Irish Poetry and the Marten Toonder Award for Literature. John F. Deane is a member of Aosdána, the body established by the Arts Council to honour artists 'whose work had made an outstanding contribution to the arts in Ireland.' His poetry has been shortlisted for the *Irish Times* Poetry Now Award and the T.S. Eliot Prize. In 1996 Deane was elected Secretary-General of the European Academy of Poetry. In 2007 he was made Chevalier en l'ordre des arts et des lettres by the French government.

ALSO BY JOHN F. DEANE FROM CARCANET

Dear Pilgrims (2018)
Semibreve (2015)
Snow Falling on Chestnut Hill: New & Selected Poems (2012)
Eye of the Hare (2011)
A Little Book of Hours (2008)
The Instruments of Art (2005)
Manhandling the Deity (2003)
Toccata and Fugue (2000)

Naming of the Bones

JOHN F. DEANE

CARCANET POETRY

First published in Great Britain in 2021 by
Carcanet
Alliance House, 30 Cross Street
Manchester, M2 7AQ
www.carcanet.co.uk

A CIP catalogue record for this book is
available from the British Library.

ISBN 978 1 80017 188 6

Book design by Andrew Latimer
Printed in Great Britain by SRP Ltd, Exeter, Devon

The publisher acknowledges financial
assistance from Arts Council England.

CONTENTS

Naming of the Bones

Like the Dewfall

SEND WORD

The song and its singers survive
in the suburbs of a restrained
silence; though violence and death resound,
there is chorale in the sacraments
of friendship, the tangles of language
in tenement and kitchen; bird-call
and ballad still rise from the gutters
of streets, from foundlings in the dark
underbelly of withholding faith
and blues will persist in the fertile
unfurling of soul. You the singer, we
the song, while beyond the arch of altar
a fox, gold-grit and lyrical, survivor,
is testing the imposing discord of earth…

*

Can you send word?
if not of comfort then at least
lament, that too
being word; or must it be
bloodlust, or the brain
astray under aseptic
lucency; or must word come
only with that final, missed
exhalation and the un-sensed
beginning of chill; is there a thick
and opaque pane between
now and forever, the hands
of the curdle-white blunt-faced
clock autocratic in their place?

*

The rose I planted, that
afternoon I came home
from his burial, twenty-
five years now and counting –
'dad's rose' I call it and it
straggles a little
on its thickened stock
pruned without skill
over those lonesome years;
but still, a light pink
shows through the greening
buds and the opened flower
will be a rare and lilac-blue
with a scent to die for…

*

Dusk – and compline;
from the darkening valley
comes the sudden
nunc dimittis servum
high-pitched cry
of the curlew, and I see
monks of those far-off
dimly-lit centuries long
gone, rise free
of the demands
of this day's wanting
and turn to spread
great grey wings, according
to your word, in peace…

*

The wild meadow is awash
with a yellow spray of buttercups;
swallows, that come swooping low
over wind-blown grasses, are shearwaters
banking over life-giving waves;
in the deep meadow, there are bubbles of lush
white and purple clovers; the chick skylarks
lurk like secrets not yet told;
the roadside ditch, in feisty commonness,
swells exotic; as if, after all the years,
I had forgotten how a life will drift
past such familiar things and now,
the wind set fair, I am an ageing tar
whose craft lies rigged and waiting in the harbour…

*

You were painting the old red gate
in Drumkeelanmore a more vibrant
red; I was watching you from the house
and my heart was singing Gershwin's
'Summertime', when a red squirrel,
with its warm-rust, fire-brick body
and its terra-cotta dust-fine tail,
came tick-tack down the eucalyptus tree
and out onto the lime-green lawn,
survivor, nervy, bold; against the white
canvas of the wall, the ruby and magenta
hollyhocks you planted were a painting
by Matisse, so that I offer you, with love,
this glass of gold-white wine, in honour…

*

In the near-ignored far corner
of the yard there is a compound clustering
of most uneasy nettles: unloved,
useless, existing on dust; but the scent
is a warm-hearth scent, where the eye
of heaven comes visiting; they cry out
to us, for they are cousins in sorrow
to the woodlouse and the earwig,
to street-urchin starlings with their mimicry
and soft-flesh beak; these nettle-crowds
are green, and grey-green and dust-green-grey,
whose love-embrace brings sting and hurt; then
dry after June sunshine, they droop and wilt,
like standing ladies discarded on the dancefloor…

*

Over the dark on-flowing of the river towards
Clew Bay, like black chestnuts or death's head
on the high wind-shaken branches, the crows –
rook and carrion, monkish and clown jackdaw –
insist on their raucous sermonizing, one
to another in caw-words, unmusical, echoing,
in their own church, structured and unreasoning,
hallowed between street and sky, above roof
and scuttling umbrellas, bustleabout deliveries,
their clusters of twig-nests, their births, marriages
and deaths, independent of the tolling of bells
or the architecture of spires; in their dark feathers
and warrior eyes, the fluctuant centuries, the millennia;
and still the crow makes wing to the rooky wood…

BY-THE-WIND SAILOR

Send forth your spirit and they shall be created,
and you will renew the face of the earth.

In the beginning, breath agitated like the breeze,
the stitched sheet rippled like a foal, and the home-built

'Unsafe' safe, craft for the now, shivering beyond the stones;
wind slight, the bog-lake standing at ease. We are children,

always, attentive to the breath. Braced
for the extraordinary.

*

In the enclosed garden there is the high proud mastery
of hollyhock and delphinium, of soft-pink rose and lupin

where bumble-bee and variegated Eden-coloured butterflies
speak ease and silence and the passion of earthen things.

Outside the walls there is the wilful human violence, darkness
of the common soul, of the quick and the departed.

Belief, with its creel of ritual and mystery, becomes
difficult. The walls are coloured with the figures of dread:

dragons and demons, the cockerel betrayal of the Christ,
barbarian terror abroad. Our breath is prayer, lifting our spirits

to the breeze. We sing our hymns to the candle-flame
and sink, all of us, refugees, into moth-silent night.

*

The mind, mornings, waits scraggy as the heron's nest
high in the ruffled treetops;

the boy in me wants to be an old-timer
riding a palomino across high sierras, inhaling orange dust

with vultures circling on the wheels of air above,
wants to be the suave and grease-haired

still-young and disillusioned toreador sipping chilled
Marqués de Cáceres rosé wine on a Toledo terrace.

*

You I think of as a bird, of a white so pure
you skim to invisibility; you are the high-pitched buzz

of the hover-fly, bog cotton in sunlight and a gusting wind,
a wavering of white butterflies struggling towards flight;

you are the Portuguese man o' war, the sea raft
wafting on the surface of the ocean, you are primordial

waters, as if the words might come *ex nihilo*, a wind
blowing across the deep, making a covenant with being.

*

Something of Yeshua/Jesus has left its caul
in my flesh, my skull is riven with a blood-feud darkness

like the painfilled leftover reek in an ancient beehive cell.
Child years were a haze of fragrances: frankincense, myrrh,

the perfumes of papa God's bazaars;
the thurible, with its chains, its censer, its incense boat

was a charmed Aladdin's lamp. I must be contented now
with homeliness from those deckled years – with peace

before high windows, wet sunlight coming through in shards
like hollyhock and soft-pink rose, Chagall-blue lupin;

I find acceptance these days amongst benevolent spectres
who have stepped beside me; and am contented with the beloved

lately dead who drift away from my mourning into the saffron-bright,
woodbine-scented morning of their all-knowing.

*

Sometimes the words caught steady brightness
though more often they languished in an under-the-stairs

dust-dark. Braced for the extraordinary I held belief
in sunlight and sacrament, in white sheets strung

along blue skipping-rope, hoisted high in sea-shore winds;
I prayed for an outpouring, *coram Deo*, the keen presence

of the breath of life, the way the Spirit came whispering fire
to the churches, that Spirit, more gannet perhaps than dove,

that white-flash down-dive welcome and daunting. Years
I have been cassocked in darkness, surpliced in light –

held safe in spite of repeated under-the-skin infidelities –
my world like the glass snow-globe that – when you turned it

upside-down – sent a tiny full-rigged ship in gentle motion
across a wavering sea. I think, now, of that innocence, moments

like a small child's small flowered wellingtons splashing
on the sky that mirrors itself in a snow-melt pool.

*

I walked, one clarifying day, the pebbled and billion-shelled
shore of the lake where you knelt, Yeshua, at dawn, preparing fish,

rewriting the landscape, redressing our suppositions
and all our certainties. You, fox on the margins, Jesus, alert

and espied. I inhaled the moon over Hermon that was duck-down white
and I drank cold beer on the shore of Kinnaret

while Israeli jets jarred the sky in their war-games,
above you – gentle and all-suffering – still – the Christ.

*

In the plum-blue out-there darkness
and high above the intently-watching towers –

in slow ballet: the galaxies, driven and intent like those
myriads of by-the-wind-sailors on the seas and can you sense

the fissures and glaciations down the faces of the planets
that are, up there, in the dance, serene. I am at home

with heather-tuft and turf-bank, with curlew-call
and the constant love-nothings murmured to the coast

by soft-capped waves. There is an old fragility
in the lace-like edges of all things, and how the solitary haw

(with its invisible, roseate angels, its prickly littlepeople)
is shot through with ivy. Tonight the constellations

will appear in another quarter of the sky, my bones
will singe with sentience of seasoning, of now, of geologic time.

I would share, down here, in the gentle communion of saints,
as the quizzical light the moon has focused on the park

will be gone by morning, the trail the vixen left through the grasses
will vanish soon, earth shriven again by her golden ochre light.

*

I watch out now over Lake Michigan; in me there is
a willingness to let go, a readiness to open to the pulse

that will touch on silence beyond silence, where word
has taken root, to reach a faith beyond faith where Word –

unheard – responds. There was a day above Keem Bay –
can you paint a beach in cobalt blue? – for there they were,

innumerable, by-the-wind-sailors, flung ashore by the high tide;
it was an image of sky, cerulean blue and shivering, a whole

testament of ages, of life and blessed passivity, words
of the world's dramas, its epics and illustrated books

where we, at our very best, discover ourselves, too,
mendicants, loving the absence that will come to save us.

*

On the hundred and somethingth floor of the Willis Tower
it is hard to breathe; you may step out here onto the skydeck,

you are straw-in-the-wind a while, open to it, and scared;
you are beyond your capacity to be and only Spirit

keeps you exposed, open to the demands of word and Word
till your being brims and overflows. You are urged back

to earth, at the sea's edge, and the spirit sighs within you;
here the black rocks are charred with weed, sheen with sea-water –

a seal, lifting its great attentive eyes, comes curious towards you,
its sleek eel-sinewy body graced under the surface, then

turns and dives back into its element, leaving you solitary again.
You have learned it, this-world wonder and danger, reach, withdrawal;

you are by-the-wind Sailor: deep blue, amethyst and cobalt,
small spirit-sail that lifts and carries you and you do not know

from where it comes nor in what station it will abandon you;
there will be disturbance at sea, touching on islands,

and millions of them – *vellela vellela* – moved by the breath,
open to it, will stir with a shiver of anticipation, breeze

soundfull, and in unison, like words that are gathering
in a chant of praise, or in a psalm, an *Eloi Eloi…* and you

are driven by gusts, gasped or long-haul, towards shore
till at last, shockingly, the whole beach is written over blue.

SAFE PASSAGE

'The isle is full of noises,
Sounds, and sweet airs that give delight and hurt not.'
– Shakespeare

'I am a body, this
is an island'
– Rowan Williams

'They lift up their voices, they sing for joy;
they shout from the west over the majesty of the Lord.
Therefore in the east give glory to the Lord;
in the islands of the sea glorify the name of the Lord.'
– Isaiah 24.

OLD BONES

I, John, I was on the island called Inishmurray…

There was a sense of Genesis to it, Alpha moment,
morning sun over the waters off Mullaghmore, boat-engine idling
while we sat on fishing-boxes
and relished the yapping of waves against the hull.

Benbulben in the distance, slopes of sun and shadow,
sheltering Ireland's poet under her wings.
The castle, Classiebawn, loomed
as a dark landmark above the cliff, and we knew

these waters brimmed, not long ago, with broken thwarts
and exploded faith. For this is Ireland, holding her wars,
her poets, her ruins and her rains, and the holy islands
where we, the curious, come to pray.

*

Outside the harbour wall we pitched in unexpected swell,
Atlantic Ocean spray
blessing us with salt. Our touching on the island was
uneasy, without dock or quay, only the black rocks

slippery with weed and sea-wet. Herring-gulls barked
like guard-dogs and a kestrel,
fast as a prayer, flew by. I scaled a rock-trail through thistles
where the testy ghosts

wished to be left in peace. To this abandonment, friars came
centuries after the Christ, to forge
salvation, built rock altars, beehive cells, stone churches,
piled up their cursing-stones to keep

*

women and fiends at bay…
What is it, then, of sea and sky and island,
of isolation and self-denial, that has left its caul
in my flesh and soul that I come

to scavenge here for understanding?
The black-backs watch, sharp-eyed and silent, shuffling
on the dry-stone walls, like monks restless in choir.
Within the ramparts of the enclosure

I sit, lost and at home. Out on the headland an old man plays,
off-tune, a slow lament:
'*an raibh tú ag an gcarraig*' and the sea responds:
a sigh and a withdrawal.

KESTREL

Vigilante couchant on a pillow of air
at-hover in the Hopkins-eye; excess of fire, self-contained, prone
to set the heather steppes ablaze:

Rufus Raptor, of the Falcon Family,
master of the chimney-stack, mistress of the house-sparrows
flustering beneath in the gutter-dust;

Prospero of the island, of moorland and coast,
upland and down, power-bolt out of the clear blue sky on field-mouse
foraging in the fodder-grass and fescue;

colour of the autumn rust-ferns,
blackspot, buff, all mastery: will rook the rook of its twig-nest,
out-pie the magpie;

nothing personal in it, no anger, no lament,
goes courting over the fall of the sea-face; 'til soon there will be
three squinching raptors, fluffy-fresh

and steel-boned, infant bill-hook
of a hook-bill. Kestrel as fact, as sunlight and storm,
as feature of island, sharpener

of the silence, tumult of the Lord
lordly in this soul scape, thunder-light on the sea-stack, a monk
in tears, huddled under the cold and the coming dark.

A SINGULAR VOICE

The old font still stands: back of the church, in a dry
stillness. I have grown old, imperceptibly, a little

cranky, but remembering how once, here, unmeasured
gifts and demands were offered me. Safe passage.

I have since learned I was not born with darkness
shadowing my soul, nor was there shame laid on me

from millennia before my birth. I am Yeshua / Jesus,
being held, then, and now, naked, in the river, angels

hovering about me: (Ted and Nanna, Jo and Don, Patricia,
big brother Declan) until the water-god released me

into order, giving me a name. Islandman, creature
of the seemly earth, here at the boundary shore of being.

They dried me off, called me Christian, wrapped me
in the whitest shawl, brought me out where thorn bushes

stood up bare in winter frost, to the potency of love
and a blessed creation. I sense they may be gathering again,

near the fount; I offer small lights and pray I may be granted *safe
passage* one more time. Outside I heard the lingering

whistle-cry of the whimbrel, a singular voice from that old
migratory bird, calling from the marshes down along the shore.

THE HUMMING TOP

Mother knelt by my crib and prayed, and I
was forgiven the sins of the day;
she blew out the flame, left me
and I was not scared of demon-dreams or the dark;

crossing my arms over my breast, I remembered
the spinning-top left downstairs, how its pictures
of horses and parrots and caravans
blurred into yellows and reds; I slept, the spinning

globe in my mind, and all of the creatures.
Though I knew how beautiful the world is,
was aware that both child and adult weep
sometimes, and though I saw how the white-fronted geese

labour through the ice-green twilight,
and watched how the robin comes brazen
to the garden seat, no one had given me
the words. And because I sensed that the dream was me

and not me, I cried too, I laughed
and made signs, knowing already
how the great world turns, and spins,
the colours fuse, and the humming goes on and on.

FOUND IN THE MARGINS: 6TH CENTURY

Today there was silence and sibilance in the scriptorium;
Brother Conall's tongue was out, moving right to left,
brushing against his teeth. Outside, dear Brother Fergus

hummed, loudly, in the barnspace, labouring
at the brewing of a strong ale; there is smell of mutton
from Brother Eogan's kitchen. Some days I am aware

that this is island, and I am island, the Devil herself
– as always – scouring the darker spaces, stables, cellars –
for this, at times, is hell and it is harrowing.

Down by the shore a craftsman is shaping stone,
chipping and chipping till the Crucified is outlined;
I think of the years ahead and the precise chiselling,

crafting to perfection. Faith is something like the sea,
gnawing and withdrawing, or something like the moon
when clouds part, then thicken again. Afternoon I saw

smoke rise like soft-winged birds from Brother Fiachra's
fire: monastery detritus – hair from old tonsured heads,
spoiled pages, kitchen orts, torn vows... I hoped to see

the Sacred Ghost hovering, but it was merely the kestrel
wrecking the carcass of a hare. Psalming is a rasping thing
like waves against fissured rocks, where fountains of sea-spray

flourish for instants on the surfaces, then worry down
in gurgles, swallows, sighs; sounding like prayers. Sheer will
sustains me on the island, keeps my shivering goose quill

scraping at the page. Last night, psalter and sackcloth and cowl
felt like fire about me and I cast them off in anger; my soul,
sinking through dark water, down to unloving depths.

THE SHOALS

Sometimes, along these storm-shattered shores,
the monks found gifts of flotsam: staves for the fires,
chattels and goods from the world of grasp
and plunder. Sometimes, too, a human frame

tangled in ropes or tattered fishing-nets. The monks
blessed them, like new-borns, with holy water,
they knelt a while and prayed, dug
graves on the further headland, marked them out

with stones and gave them names: *Alma, Magnus, Nox...*
They wrapped what was left of body
in a winding-sheet while their God stood over all,
harvesting in love and sorrow the many worlds

he had created, spirits shoaling through space like herring,
the souls of the monks blown about in the winds.

DEAD MAN'S BOOTLACES

Iona

Here you will walk on clover to the white beach,
over tiny cowrie shells, gold-orange

like curlicues from the Book of Kells;
you will stand in the lightness of sea-water

that comes murmuring over ivory-coloured sand,
feet bare to the sand-eels that caress your skin,

see them swirl in the water like little l's of water
while their shadow-lines beneath them seem

more substantive than they. The stones are the tears
of Saint Columba: dark green for the loss of Ireland,

translucency for the soul in grief, serpentine for treachery.
Cache of the shore-line: sea-weed allsorts, weeds wavery

like mermaids' scarves, dead man's bootlaces, stones
like mottled eggs of the wren and ostrich, bracken

with its petulant browns, its roistering and its lettering.
There are boulders, blunt as the head of a whale, pebbles

and parti-coloured shells, child's treasure-hoard. Worlds
like the wonder and mystery of a cosmic, a scripted, Word.

ON A GRASSY SLOPE

Iona

There is a hidden cove
with an egret-white carpet of sand; there are
sea-sounds, from bass drum roll
to New World oboe. The undertow spreads out
a delicate talcum-soft sea-dust
through the purest blue of ocean. The cove
sighs softly in amazement at itself, cosmos
extant in every grain, shifted and sifted by out-tide
and return. On three sides the sea-rock walls
have been gnawed for centuries;
on the headland, a rusted crane
stands, neck and beak – stork-like – raised
in patterns of rust and black, its hanging chain
hoists nothing
up from nowhere, down to nowhere;
and will, with all flesh, flake itself into sky
over the aeons, and disappear.
I sit a long while, between
headland and cove, between
time and time, where nothing unexpected
will take place, though the air is close
with alteration, my inhaled breath, exhaled.

DOGWOOD

Iona

The monks, Celtic warriors for Christ, suffered
the impossible monotony of the hours – moving
in a shuffle-silence, cowled ghostly figures shifting

towards office. Antiphonal responses rose at times
sharp as the crying of seabirds. Thoughts swirled
like gnats, itching with an eager devilish nastiness.

In the profound dark beyond midnight, what sounds
save those of mischief? Still were they undaunted
in the pursuit of wisdom. Wisdom always like mist

ahead and out of clutch. How is it possible to continue?
Matins, to lauds, vespers, compline. Hard to hold
that the overarching God was primed to pleasure

from their often off-tune lauds. They gnawed on the flesh
of the God-Son, filching a tiny flouring of divinity,
they sipped a little of the wine-wild madness

of the Godhead. At the heart of nothingness, *point
vierge*, there is the contained fire of devastated love.
Days of dogwood and dearth. Of sackcloth and strong ale.

Though the spirit sagged like sodden clothes hung out
along a rope, they persisted in illuminating the bright Book
of Hours, serpents on one folio, angels on the next.

THE FLOWERING

In the convent halls, religious order;
in the nun's garden, a riotous abundance;

in the parlour she is offering a tray, with coffee, tea,
biscuits plain and chocolate-chip;

at the garden's edge, the boiler room – boots
with soft clay drying to a grey daub – and the instruments:

trowel and secateurs, gardening gloves and kneelers. Then
she is out – forget-me-not-blue apron over navy habit –

and she moves, like a ward sister, working to tend,
to prune, to coax; kneels, as if in prayer, 'concerning

the times and seasons', evening primrose, flowering
sage, Siberian wall-flowers. The high iris stands,

an extravagantly coiffed princess, by the sapphire-coloured rose;
nearby, flowers she cares for, with names like those of exotic

foreign traders: alium, astrantia, delphinium; they lift
in homage to kindly, ministering hands, hands that fold, often,

in pleading. To-night she will sit a while, after Vespers, alone
on the wrought-iron garden seat, and will be glad –

thinking of bridal bouquet, corsage, ring –
that soon she will stumble away into that old, singular garden

to meet, at last, the Bridegroom, to yield
to the drag of origins within, to her own, certain, flowering.

LINDISFARNE

To-night the sea, out in the obdurate dark, shifts
in obedience, the seals hauling themselves out
onto the long shelf of sand, in their own slick nudity,

shifting, too, in a restlessness of seals, their plangent
hymns to one another carrying into the weave of human
dreams and half-sleep, into the flesh of the long dead

floating in dust of the universe in soul-nakedness.
We are young a while, and seek sanctuary, Lindisfarne,
where saintly ghosts glide by, their voices distant

as the loon's song out over the ocean, and close
as the curlew's call purling from the fens.
The North Sea's force spends itself in spume

and the herring-boats lie safe above the tide-line.
I seek a haven that is not loneliness but a table
set with a white linen nappe and laid for four.

We will be old a time, allowed some scope, hold
that the poems shaping themselves in the soul's sanctum
may stay the waves a while as they call out to our God.

I AM

I left the pew, slowly, following
men and women old as I, and older;
we are cautious now, we – communion

of the living – holding on. I took
in my palm the white, the cosmic bread
and placed it on my tongue, took a sip

of the earth-sweet and bitter wine;
amen, I said, amen. So am I guest
at the crude table of the Upper Room,

am Jewish-Christian, Hellenist, I am
Greco-Roman, Byzantine, bear on my tongue
full two millennia of a difficult history,

the proving – down a long bleak tunnel
scarce candle-lit – of the original mandate
of the Alpha, the Omega Christ.

AIDAN: A LIFE

Connacht born, lean and intent, he prayed –
may all that you are, Jesus, live in me;

child-spine already strengthening upwards, he reached
for the strict and straitened life of islands –

the Arans, Iona, Lindisfarne. He would be
adept in new languages, out of Gaelic into English,

out of flesh and into Jesus. He grew itinerant,
travelling through the smalltowns, fishing villages,

a black flame visible along the causeway, embracing
the Christ-fire to his chest. Autumn, and festival,

foison in the fields and villages, apples, hazels, farm-scents,
calls of the Brent geese from the marshes, flotillas

of Eider riding the inshore waves; and Aidan's harvesting
rising slowly to heaven like a white smoke, because the last

of this earth's people, caps in hand, expect for themselves
no miracles, only their daily bread, a modicum of peace.

CUTHBERT: A LIFE

Through chill and warmth in the low hills
he learned the music timid sheep respond to:
that soft and ululating boy-song

of artlessness and sweet grass, a high-pitched
guardian air that drove the falcons
far from the brimming harmlessness of lamb.

He was taken from innocence too young.
At twelve, apprenticed to a saint. Life
over. Harshness was a creed and habitude.

He walked the earth on muddy, rutted trails,
tramping hillock, hollow and lane, handling
immensities. By offal pits and slurries

he confessed our immortality. Shepherding.
Solicitous, not for this life, but for treasure
in heaven. What then, Cuthbert,

of the poor and ignorant,
intimates of this world of grace and ugliness,
what of the body, dear and beautiful,

what of the Christ of banquets, what can you say
of God's most good creation? And what
of eros, and the waiting arms of the love-lorn Christ?

COLMÁN ON LINDISFARNE

In the un-night, un-dawn, not-light, I lay
face down on the painfulness of stones

and knew the dampness of the ebb-tide sea
seep to my flesh and nothing could I pray, no word, no

sap in me, the long dryness and emptiness of me
so great a sore I could deny all life and more –
my Jesus!

when somewhere near, at the limits of village,
the proud-shrill cackle-cry rise-and-fall of the rooster's

cock-crow tenor and bass times three and the tears at last came
loosening me and the word came, just – the one word –
Christus

and I think I passed into an un-sleep un-
waking dream because I stirred and there was light and a hard

stiffness in my bones, and I saw the fox so startled it dropped
the bloodied, head-lost carcass of the cock, dropped it

down on stones beyond me and loped, surlily, back
into the scrub-brush and so I took

the feather-sticky brokenness and gashed-open
hot-bloodied creature in my hands and knew, for once,

in the feel of the ebbing and stilling of the heart, I knew
all of it, the violence and sorrow of the spirit, the joy

and exuberance of benevolence, raptor and prey all-in-one
like the vision of the risen Jesus water-walking

through the deepest reaches of my soul so close
I could ease my finger to the sticky blood of his holed feet,

see the tiny crumbs spring off in the breaking of the bread
and I whispered Colmán I whispered Colmán let
go and let go let

be and let be, in the wholeness of the origin of love
and its destination in the wholeness of the convergence of all things.

SLOWDANCING: INISHBOFIN

Come now into the west, in late May sunshine
when fields are warm with the goldlight of buttercup and furze;

take ferry to the island, where you will find the sky
of a high and perfect blue; Atlantic, you might think,

will be smooth and sparkling, all the way to the Americas.
Old-time trawlers lean, at rest, ragged epics of survival

and disaster, of the infidelities of ocean. The island hymns,
out by the side of things, its small fields graced for centuries

by the same stone walls, the off-tune calling of the landrail,
the flourishing wild columbine. You have been passing borders,

and crossing over; you will be witness to Colmán's church,
a presence in this old all-hallowed ground; in our later age,

there is only the soft sighing of the wind, in the remote privacy
that is death. Under your feet, under grass and clay, the dust

of the once-graced slowdancers of a dedicated faith, outside time,
where the mystery was suffered, and love attempted. Soon you are

ripe for evening and the restaurant, lit; there will be mussels, lobster,
a fine Rioja white, lace table-cloths, and a soft, agreeable chattering.

THE RATTLE OF OLD BONES

The men were standing outside the church, hearing
Mass; dark Sunday suits, flat caps and cautionary pipes;

serious men, one eye on weathers, one on neighbours,
easing this hour between worlds, jocular, strong-jawed

and firm-standing, like erratics. In St Colmán's
ruined monastery, sheep safely graze; in waves off-shore

the fishing-boats chant, in old Gaelic, timeworn psalms
of the wild-weltering sea. In deepest hour of night, the bones

of monks, slaughtered in the malevolent invasions
of the Vikings, set themselves to their eight-hand reels,

there is joy through communion of saints, out under the light
of the moon – spine-slides, skeletal slip-jigs, the hysterical

laughter of skulls. 'Woe is me,' saith the book, 'for my soul
hath fainted, because of the saints that are slain.'

DEATH LULLABY

Gabriel Fauré

There is a worldly holiness to it, the piano, closed,
a corner of the parlour mirrored in its polished wood.

He sits a while, waiting; when he closes his eyes he hears
music somewhere above the city, the roofs of Paris

catching a white light from the moon's pale watching.
To open the chapel doors of the instrument is to release

the spirit, that comes stirring where it wills and will not tell
its source, nor destination. He writes it first at the piano:

heart to soul, to mind and fingertips, wishing to send it
through to the other side, notes to the loved and gone,

envying the one who has discovered, at last, all truth and beauty.
He remembers that coward school-child before the bullies,

the Croix de Guerre after the Commune. After war, after a death,
what has been mellifluous will grow sombre. How, after love's failure,

write of tenderness? and after Wagner, how write at all? Fauré
plays as if the ivories were silk, the ebonies sable, his

Kyrie a kiss, his *requiescat* a finger-touch, his *miserere* an embrace;
Pie Jesú, the spirit breathes, and then at last *in paradisum deducant te*

angeli, spirit, *pianissimo*, acceptance almost, the after-silence
lingering long, something accomplished, something achieved.

FOOD FOR THE JOURNEY

It felt like an old-style railway-station, sunlight
slanting in onto drabness, older people
sitting in discomfort; outside, the ocean heaved as usual,
the sky was clear, one white cloud hung, watchful.
They drew down the blind as if the sacrament of his going
might fructify only in darkness. Old man in extremis,
stubble in the runnels of his face, and – in candle-light
by the bedside – old-man breath like a moth hovering
near the flame. The priest, solemn in cassock and surplice;
yellow-wax candles on a white-clothed table-top, a crucifix,
a blue jug, white cloth – all this, almost too much after a life
of difficult labour. You could hear the piercing calls
of the whimbrel, the snickering of gulls. The priest
murmured Latin words, prayed that the soft-snow Eucharist,
placed on his tongue, might keep him from the malignant
foe. The old man breathed a little easier, the priest, pleased,
stood a while, nodded, turned and went out. The old woman
stood quiet, who has passed through the tedious rosaries
of the seasons; she will be self-contained again
after the going, become island, will shift, mornings,
chipped blue china on the sagging shelves. Outside, the tide
had brimmed, would soon stir again and begin to ebb.

CROSSING THE SAND

At times the sand, settled after winds, is white
as a meadowscape of snow;
here is the boundary of the inhabited world, the sea
cerulean, eelgrass of the dunes

coarse as stubble on the old man's
pallid face.
For years you could have seen him labouring
with others, hoisting the curragh on strong shoulders

and stepping under, trudging across the sand –
like some large and millipeded insect – slowly
towards the waves.
Nights sometimes, with the sea pounding the rocks outside,

rain flinging itself against the windows,
voices rose, hoarsely, to the *Salve Regina:*
our life, our sweetness, and our hope, then sank again:
and after this our exile… Six men, soon, will hoist

the coffin on strong shoulders, and stepping under
will trudge out across the sand,
leaving deep footprints and moving, slowly
down towards the ever-churning sea.

NEAR RESTFUL WATERS

I think I could stand here for a day, and for always.
There are two
weathered-white and unkempt cart-horses
– grazily – in a bedraggled field, watching; there are

patches of the purple lace-cap grannie hydrangeas
frowzy now, drooping
dishevelled, and a rioting in corners
of the sweet-pink wild dog rose. The heathlands

stretch in ease towards the scattered hills
quilted with rocks,
with corries and autumn heathers. Nothing
stirs; the stream that lazed through the summer ground

is clogged with briars and ragged Joseph lilies.
Still, all around me, lie
the congregations, widows, widowers, the young and not-so,
grandfather Ted left lone in a large plot, godmother

Patricia (young, too-young) in her single bed – the long sadness
forever hovering –
and the crosses, stone and makeshift, that lean and reach
in this jumble-world of the island dead. The old ones, in their day,

told how the mysteries abound, the way pure spring water
comes whispering
from ferns and cresses, cool through lime-washed stones
in deep wells. I could stand here under the sly insinuations

of a transparent moon, could watch this tousled bunch of plum
clouds on the horizon,
everything comfortably rumpled: as if structure and point
were of no import, just this now, this here, sufficient unto itself.

BILBERRY BELLS AND ASPHODEL

This is the yellow house where the dead
return, rehearsing their old delights, bemoaning the loss
of rough-red Lifebuoy soap against the skin,

or the heat against her knuckles as Grandmother Nora toasts
bread on the long fork held to the fire; Grandfather Ted
misses the drool of melting butter along the hot

potato boxty cake, and oh! how Father
longs for the slow-walk down to the well to dip the jug
with its blue-rose pattern, and hear the first

flush-slap of water into the dinted, off-white pail.
You too, brother, do you sense it, sunlight
flickering on fern, on bilberry bells and asphodel,

those wander-lust mornings we heard the hum of insects
and the fuzzy sounds of bees busy inside the blossoms?
And do you remember – now that you too

have gone into the world of light – how we sat on our hard
three-legged stools and sang, there in the corner
by the high fuchsia and the rhododendron, *All things bright*

and beautiful? Will you come back, now, to pick up once more
words of the yellowhammer's song, that smell from pages
of the new reader with the odour of apples baking in the kitchen,

while Mother's welcoming arms waited for an embrace?
How fine then the weight of knowledge, like featherfall,
and we, content in our unknowing, in our young otherselves!

WOOD

Grandfather Ted could turn his hand
to everything: lathe, plane or blade; his finished
mahogany sideboard
wore delicately-fretworked knobbles, curlicues and scrolls,

burnished to a dark perfection. It was devotion
that excluded all others. Yet Grandmother Nora
knew how he loved her,
he simply could not frame the words, nor,

in those darkling and unsuspecting years, did he know
to show affection. Evenings
he smoked, briar pipe sheened and polished to an exquisite
handling; he was gathering himself

to a luxurious isolation. Afterwards he sighed,
wrapping away the briar in a smooth-running, locked drawer
of the precious sideboard. When he died
(and was carried out in a wood-sheened brass-handled

treasure-chest) Nora
found woodworm ravaging the furniture
and small teeth-marks disfiguring
the lustrous stem of his briar-wood pipe.

GRANDFATHER TED / JOHN CONNORS

I

Take the lane, left off the road, turn
a corner, off a corner, down a strait, dirt track –
the Bunnacurry graveyard;

here is portal, frontier, that holds
in the depths of its gravities
root of our making, ancestry, and stock.

A horse, ragged and mud-caked
and frisky with horse-life,
whinnies loudly from across a field,

while something in me is tethered
to this near-lost out-of-the-way corner
of the cosmos, something of me

beached on this island strand,
like a clinker-built row-boat with its boards
splintered, diminishing in the winds.

11

Dear Jackie:

Because you asked.
I had grown old and crusty when you knew me, frail as old parchment, as a frost-encrusted eucalyptus tree. You might peel away the papery outer layers, peel back layer upon tear-making layer, and I am the song of childhood, wise in the knowledge of nothing, quick in the fling of the body; but then, when you knew me, there was nothing left to be peeled away. My life was scribbled in ridges and furrows across the permanent stubble of my jaw. I was stiff, I feared I might crack. I tapped the bowl of my pipe against the mantel, my knee leaned hard against the bars of the fire and I shrank with the pain. I entered – an atrium, resentful at first of the great confusion and suffering and then – resentful of morphine and of comfort words, the intrusions of language, the impositions of care. World, weathers, wars – irrelevant then as newspaper pages blackening and blowing away in a backyard fire. I held my body still and hard, in preparation. Thus; on fire; for nights; and days. Something like peace, once, a moment perhaps, perhaps an hour; I knew her again, Nora, your grandmother, lips on my brow, fingers like dewfall on my cheeks. Then monotonous, sea-wave intoning of rosaries. But I was grateful beyond grief or pain, merely tired. Incapable of stirring to her, of opening lips, or eyes. But her love had pierced me. I remembered the crucified. I confessed. In my blood. I flared, quietly, into the process.
Yours,
John Connors

III

There is a touch, in the graveyard,
of the primal garden, its rusted, un-kept gate,
its leisurely lopsided lean,
sea-shell patterns and sea-pebbles on grave and gravestone,

I knelt to pray; to you, beyond father, beyond life,
beyond reach – and still I pray…
Old Ireland. Old Gentleman, Grandfather,
barely extant in memory,

like shoots unclutching from their place.
Sometimes I believe in the One,
the blood-giver, the laughter-maker
and the one – with you on the other side of hereness,

her well-loved warrior-virgin face
alight in joy and expectation: here,
where the robin chitters without chariness
from the branches of the blackthorn,

and the lilac-purple
blossom-flames of the foxglove
bend double in the bracken under gale-force winds
and straighten again, unquenchable.

IV

Dear Jackie:
Because you asked;
Where I am now, I am Guardian, a light directing a star through the darkness of a winter wood, the constellations around innumerable, like the varieties of melody and bird-song in the old world. I am guiding my charge towards harbour. It is the beauty of the darkness enthrals me, for I am light. I guide my craft through the blackness of the ocean that is space, my being suffused with joy, an ocean where I am alone save for the over-abundant all-love of my God, am spirit to the matter that is moving ever towards the final harmony. I am God's son embraced on the waters. And though I soar alone, I am encompassed always by your grandmother, Nora the beloved, by Patricia, Jim and Jack, by your mother Jo, your father, Don, by Declan, by your good friends Herbert, Hopkins, Heaney – by an innumerable multitude from all the ages and all the nations. Because I am island still, though more so: pebble to the Atlantic Ocean, sand-grain to the Pacific: and every particle holds all others, and every particle is filled with the existing of God. Exult with me, boy, exult in joy and understanding.

Your affectionate grandfather,
John

V

I knelt, on damp grass, anywhere between past and future;
I could hear the children playing in the school-yard

and heard the bell call angelus from the monastery tower,
I said the prayer, forgetting that the monastery

lies in lichened ruins and the school has long since crumbled
into dust. I could see the fields and ditches sloping

upwards, the ocean, to the right, and quiet; I saw the clouds,
darkening and ominous, slung on the shoulders of Slieve
        More;

I crave confirmation, what there is of you, Grandfather Ted,
in me, you, up-stiff and straight, with rule and T-square,

back-of-the-house craftsman, withdrawn
from gaiety, old man of ritual, salt and righteousness.

VI

Dear John,
Because you did ask!
You called out once, out of nightmare, and I yielded. It was I went to your room and held your small, sweet-smelling body against my own bruised, old-century self; for such a time I held you, only the light from remote galaxies softening the blackness and a night-bird somewhere across the fields, calling out, as you had, in some real, or feared, distress; until you slept, the easiest of child-smiles on your lips, but I did not want to lay you down, your being blessing mine. And I felt safe, at last, rescued by an access of love, and the world turned, and I let go of my rage and hollowness. I heard in your breathing the voices of the earth and could accept the forces of movement that are greater than myself. I laid you down, I went back to your grandmother. So, dear John: this I say, quiet now your soul; for they are quiet, quiet the sea, the air, the mountains, the heavens; quiet, as after a winter gale, the sun risen, the sea sparkling. The Holy Spirit stirs across the universe, in a power-filled quiet. The Christ, of whom you – being conscious of fault – are wary, moves in loving strides, through the creation. There is love vast as the cosmos, intimate as a hug. Christ's life is your life, the Spirit draws on you, you are part of the growing and the growing is part of you. I kept a many-coloured globe of the world on the upstairs landing, do you remember it? and we turned it about together, sometimes, when you came from school. I wound the eight-day clock each Sunday evening, and you offered to help, but I would not let you. See, now, there are lichens and green-moss coins along my gravestone and they are tinged with the allness of God, the little pimpernels stand stronger, more fluent than rose or daffodil, and they, too, play their part. Kneel, then, if you will, though the grass is damp. But keep the words still within you. Listen, rather. Listen. Be.

Your ever loving grandfather Ted.

THE WALL

Summer weather, and she stood – widowed – watching,
her face taut in a new depth of stillness, grey hair, heavy

body, there and, for a moment, shadowed by something
I could not surmise. Did I gain knowledge then, registering

some pit of silence beneath the child-calls of our play,
and did I stop a moment in my gambolling, smitten?

The front door stood half-opened into darkness near her,
a honey-cold gleam fell on the yellow-frosted arched windows

to either side; the garden was hedged by the waxy green of
escallonia, dressed with the amber leaning of gladioli, and she –

stricken with years – leant against the wall of the house, arms
folded, fleshed as I thought like the spoiling of snow.

The others (and who they were) are as ghosts at the edge,
non-being to the instant of my being, till it began again, like

water that might have stalled as it poured out of a jug, then went on
falling, or as if lace curtains had fluttered a moment in an upstairs

window, revealing a pained face watching: I the reality, all things else
unreal. I hold it, in all the weathers of my being, and know

how images fade into a grieved absence, how my hurting arms
would comfort her, as I reach out now towards a lost radiance.

ACCOMPANIED

The ascent is easiest at the beginning;
six men, strong labourers,
right-shoulder left-shoulder,
take the weight; bog-path, ground rising already,

passing by the *cillín* of the lost children,
big waves bullying in
against the low-cliff home-ground
this side the mountain,

home ground too – rest eternal – the other side.
This human stream, dark-frothed,
rises slowly, against nature;
soft, almost-animal, coughs and cries

and women, shawled, huddling.
Pause;
lower the coffin carefully,
to shift the ache in the bearers' flesh;

build a small cairn of stones where the coffin touched,
a station; six fresh bearers.
On, over heath-hummock, steep bank and treacherous earth;
only the dead man peaceful and unwary.

There will be, at the top, a longer pause,
a larger cairn, a lingering look back
over the long curve of the bay, the sea breaking
audibly still, the deep past incalculable.

Beads are told, a mind-numbing, repetitious drone.
Station; six more labouring men,
left-shoulder right-shoulder,
for the more difficult descent. There are men below,

at rest on pick and shovel,
watching up at the dismal sacrament that moves
like a bleak and bog-black
sluggish watercourse, inaudible from below;

there are gulls' cries, a distant
curlew calling, the monkish
hooded crows kraaking,
and sleek black slugs mating under the rain.

ON KEEL BEACH

I bring my demons down to the sea-shore
and loose them amongst unsettling sea-rolled stones;

here I stand firm against the storm-winds, cherishing
the buffeting and the surging power of the waves, the delicate

seam-stitching needlework of receding water. Wrapped tight
in my great-coat, hands in pockets, I release the memories

and the winds will carry them away: *what*
are the wild waves saying? I sing, in the mind's recess,

sing with my brother, appeasing parents in the old sitting-room,
world gracious and at ease, turf-fire vibrant in the grate, slow,

sentimental duet – *that ever amidst our playing*
I hear but its low, lone song. Tattered along the tide-line,

refuse of the ocean: bladderwrack and wing-kelp, toxins
of our human desecration, and there – amongst the cans

and plastics – the rotting carcass, the sodden feathers
of a gannet. Out across the sea, beyond my ken

but within my prayers, sorrows and slaughters of this
still-young century; Tikrit, Mosul; the heart is wrenched

by the barbarities; Babylon and the rivers,
Tigris, sluggish now with military waste,

and the Euphrates, blue river, its waters
drying up, trickling towards a desolate sea. And I remember

father, mother, in their easy-chairs by the fire,
Granny by the window, humming, her knitting-needles

clacking their steady rhythms: *Brother, I hear no singing,*
'tis but the rolling wave. Away to my left the great, dark cliffs,

cathedral-proud, the fulmar soaring; where father fished,
spinning from the rocks for mackerel, his taut and urgent

longing, evident. And I see them, too, the children,
wretchedly clothed, in the wind-blown tents for refugees, filled

landscapes of them, snow falling, severe frost holding;
their eyes are dulled and unblinking, watching. My brother

is at peace now in the Queen of Heaven cemetery, the small
many-coloured whirling windmills humming loss. I turn

for home, old man cold and dry-eyed, remembering.
Yes! the song concluded, *but there's something greater*

that speaks to the heart alone. The voice of the great Creator
dwells in that mighty tone. And the wind turns, and the tide.

THEN AND NOW

He – abandoning the inland sureties of the Christian Brothers –
came, for the first time, to island; took up fishing from the high

rocks beyond Purteen, stirred by the wonder of the Atlantic; I,
then unthought of, am there, too, on the cliff-edge near him, waiting.

She – native to island – was picnicking, with Patricia, on the strand,
a basket with sandwiches, a rose-red wine and Waterford

cut-glass tumblers; they have been laughing, youth and promise
copious as the blue sky. I, then unthought of, am there, too,

watching from the breaking waves, waiting. Now I stand, sea's edge,
stunned at the knowledge of my ageing, he, and she, and Patricia,

decades gone into the ocean of all unknowing. And since
time itself is imagination, and then is now, now then – I call to them

from where I sit, pensive and waiting, January rain slanting down
and vanishing into the heaving sea, melding with its waves, its breakers.

WALKING THE ROADS

Or I could, perhaps, spend all there is of after-life
walking the road between Dooagh village
and the beach at Keem, flexing the spirit-muscles,

strengthening the spirit-bones. Sometimes a telephone pole,
blown over in a Force 10, lies down across the path,
communication wires from the island to the raucous world

tangled like fishing-gut. Here I have most nearly found
the source of the being of Ireland, my soil, my sky,
my sea, my here-ness. I will have learned the thousand words

that said amen to the thousand weathers I had grown
familiar with, learned to hold my breath when witnessing
the rare serene light shining over the bay, the sea

a delicate shamrock green, translucent, and the waves
fingering the slow notes of a Schubert lullaby on the strand.
Or have learned how behoving it may be to relish

the imperfect: like blood-poppies struggling for space
against hard-fisted thistles; without the breeze
how could we ever watch the sea-waves shifting

over bounteous prairies of green grass. For spirit goes on
gleaning light out of the long living, tucking it away
in nourishment, solstice, moonshine, offering it back

in poems, (small things, like quivering moths)
in the music of Brahms, in the birthing in stone
of Michelangelo, in the clear footprints of the Christ.

POSTLUDE

Today, in the marshland down by the cove,
the entire flock lifted as one; they were crying,
in anticipation of the journey, and they wheeled,
once, twice, turning above me where I stood
and coming back, low, over the feeding-grounds, then –

as if they had braced themselves – heading out over the sea.
I heard the powerful beating of their wings, one heart
holding them, one instinct guiding. I watched
'til they became a small dark stain on the horizon
that faded into distance, and silence. I stood a long time,

saddened in the aftermath. I will miss them, the easy
unmusical honking, the saffron legs, the companionable
bickering across the marshes. Tonight,
as we, one heart, shift manfully in choir, the psalm
Dixit Dominus domino meo...on our lips, the geese,

white-fronted, will be still in flight, a darkly shifting shape
outlined against the chill of the moon. And later still
I will shake off sand from my sandals, kneel a while and,
in the way of prayer, envy that homing instinct, that strength
of purpose, and enter my solitary self, my individual wilfulness.

EXILE

i.m. David Gascoyne

In an age of extraordinary desperation, grant us
extraordinary grace.

The flags are black over the pillaged cities. What I fear most
is disillusion. From the forces of evil deliver us.

We have grown lax, luxurious in our living, we have misprized
our hard-won luminosity; how then can we blame the young
for the furnaces of their yearnings?

Here, in the lethargic west, goldfinch bustle about spring business;
the hawthorn, this May time, displays a lavish whiteness;
the earth, once more, is in song, dressing itself in radiance…

But there is news of that ancient city, honoured
in its theatres and temples, where human worth
has been known valid; fury, these days,
has been feeding there on death and killing.

We learn again how the generations may surpass each other
in unnatural confusions, how the thousands
of new, wide-eyed refugees
are tossed in rusty tubs across hostile oceans – but

forgive me: it is not all darkness;

the poet, shaken by world war, wrote: *The Son of Man*
is in revolt against the god of men.

We have the ancient psalters, the beauty of illuminated Gospels,
and even now, though we know the human covenant has been
fragmented, I can say: Nevertheless!

for though the red-leaf oak, our *quercus rubra*, had lost
first leaves – shrivelled after a too-late frost – I have seen
new shoots, green-lit, swell;

and we, we will stand in community still to pray
deliver us from evil, still turn to one another,
offering a sign of peace.

REDCURRANTS

There had been catstink out by the bushes,
and I was scared
for the song-thrush, its nest
a chalice of grass and twigs, carpeted

with mud and human hairs; there were five
glossy sky-blue eggs
spotted with black stars. The birds, evenings,
intoned old Gaelic melodies

in the back yard, tenderly repeated
flute-notes, sounding
of woods and orchids and running streams.
The redcurrant bushes

had wintered like stragglers after the fair,
leftovers, wickerings,
but now are rich with leaves and hidden
currant clusters. Dandelions swarm

through the grasses and thrush's song holds
a sweeter bitterness;
thrush's young are fattening on snail and worm,
thrush has a fine red berry in its bill; and I,

in God's in-breathing out-breathing presence,
am at prayer, I am
psalm and psalter, word and silence, I am bird
and bush and berry, accompaniment and song.

TO STAND IN CHOIR

Within sheltering walls, ours is a steady and a grave
dance, for we move
scarcely at all, shuffling in place, holding safe

distance from one another, to tone cacophony
to symphony. Silence,
prayer, repudiation. The presence that – demanding – still

withholds. It is dreamlife, this immersion in the circling
seasons of the psalmody. I have news
for the world, good news, gleaned from the stubble

of sorrows, from the entangled undergrowth
of prayer. I have stumbled
onto the intersection of this world's barbarous beauty

and the misery; for this is island, and it is offshore.
I stand a while,
after the splitting of firewood, holding the axe,

relishing the thuck and shudder, the precise satisfaction;
oak and ash, like monks,
persist, bare-wintered shiverers and silence-hoarders.

I watch, by my small window, out on the flux of stars
in the risen night-winds;
in my prayers I cry to the communion of all-souls,

but my words seem spittle and my spittle dust.
A Thiarna, trócaire! Uncertainty
is the mouse that gnaws on ancient parchment beneath

the floorboards: faith may be a matter of the knuckles
whitening, of self as false notes,
well off-key. We gather driftwood, we clamp sods of turf

against a wall. We will stand exposed to the secrecies
we hold inside, listening
for the word within that silence; there will be moans, at times,

as if our ghosts were on the loose; and dread that we –
out of all hardihood – might unravel,
be puffed about like foam blowing off the ocean waves.

for Michael P. Murphy

BONEYARD

From Ireland, to Crete, island to island, a long
journey. Late in the twentieth century we believed

the medieval eons had come to an end; we were
a young country, teenagers broaching adolescence –

we spent whatever money we could marshal. Seminaries
abandoned, the starch of surplice, the surety and mindfulness

of Gregorian chant – we took to the roads and highways
to garner riches, to dine, to shine, meander. But fresh

Vikings were gathering beyond our sanctuaries, poised and
hungry for outrage. Having the new, we dismissed

the old songs. On Crete, in Orthodox peace of chant
and incense, we could recognize those who still

take God at his Word. In the monastery of Arkadi,
three monks remain, the rich catholicon holds

relicts of the priests' resistance to the Ottomans
and the Nazis, bullet-holed and sword-cut skulls

are testament to an old belief. In the dim church
we knelt, alien and at home, praying, for the worth of it,

for the century unfolding in outlandish ways, knowing
how we are halt and butt against the limitations of our words.

THE OLIVE GROVE

Sfakaki, the townland;
Rethymno, the province;
the island, Crete.

We are sitting in an olive grove,
the trees gnarled and stumped
like the centuries; the fruits, this season,

remain hard as sloes. In the distance,
southward, there are cocks
crowing, as they have always crowed;

cicadas are starting up, like the incessant ringing,
in the hallway, of an old-fashioned
telephone; a cat, under a tree,

has dozed all day, coming alive sometimes
to play at tig with a lizard, while big
stiff insects, with stilt-legs, stick-bodies

and wings of muslin, are suddenly there
where never supposed to be. We share
a warm Cretan red, and wonder idly

if the earth beneath the olive-trees
is tunnelled into labyrinths
or if a human shape, this twilight, might come

soaring from the mountain-top with sail-sewn wings.
But we rest easy, knowing that the gods
have gone to roost among the immortal dead,

and have stored away – for the moment –
their wars and rivalries,
their bacchanals.

ICARUS

Young man of the Cretan uplands, downlands,
of the labyrinthine rutways of mountain villages,
olive-groves, goats, of the gaunt, bell-ringing sheep –

he would fly, as I would, in the relish of bounteous grace.
Whipped by the wind at first, as fear will fling you,
then mastering it, the shoulder-muscles jousting;

then it was the light, blinding him as he topped
Mount Ida and the White Mountains, the island below
like rags and patches clawed and torn, strewn about.

When the blindness eased he saw Daedalus, maker-Father,
cautious on the up-draughts beneath, but by now the son
was master, beyond fear, beyond vision, climbing

on the upbeam of the sky, feathered arms spread
cruciform and soaring; so high he saw the earth revolving
and time itself like a vineyard fruiting and dying back.

So high, at last, so cold, pain suffusing, he was suffering,
punished for robbing the world of gravity, till what was glory
froze in him, bones, sinews, becoming iron, and he plummeted,

bloodless, over the utmost horizons of our history.

TRIPLE H

Sometimes I think of them, the saints:
their sutured habits and ghost-white cinctures,

eyes wide-open upwards in a static rapture, their floating
inches above the flagged floor in cantilevered ecstasy,

and the words we use: inimitable, righteous, the
un-mortals: Hippolytus, Helena, Hyacinth…

Often I think of them, the saints:
writing outside themselves of themselves inside –

Hopkins in his long, unglamorous suffering,
small snappy man in a misery of muscled language;

Herbert, his consciousness of dustworth,
his tentative but eager treaty of love;

and Heaney, witness to the gracefulness of the frames
of dailiness, enamoured of the possible, the worth

of next-door otherness and the allsorts savouring of words:
these, O God, your dead, your un-mortals.

AGEING MARINER

I, John, your brother and companion in the suffering and kingdom,
was on the island of Patmos...

At imaginable distances from the harbour, Skala,
glaciers are groaning in distress, green-blue ice
becoming ocean; and drifting; the way the silent
almost-invisible Vikings once towards Lindisfarne

breached on the shores of islands. Still
in dirt-sand corners by the tumbledown canebrakes,
old dusty dogs are chewing on their fleas, and the sea
anciently washes up debris along the pebble strand.

Under the high cold moon of intellect, we may divine
we are merely grains of cosmic ash sandwiched a while
between nothingnesses. Nevertheless I crouch, a child

high on the mast-head, watching out for land
and home, willing to live by the New Law
written on sinews of the heart by our mariner Christ.

THE MEDITERRANEAN

Here, in the fields of mercy, the spirits of those
hundreds, thousands
of children, women, men, come brushing by me,
fleeing the human hornets

of fanaticism and greed, though too many have found
quiet in the bitter depths
of the Mediterranean Sea – who will, one day, rise again
to the surface, children, women, men

with psalms accusatory on their lips. Now I stand
on the sheltered island coast, the sea
brushing the shore softly; I am awed by the yellow-linen
stillness of evening primrose, and by butterflies

storming the buddleia, while the star-shaped
golden-white geranium is wilting
in its pot. Ageing body, dull brain perplexed,
I am startled by the scream of a black-back

carrion gull and can image the over-crowded tubs
and rusting wrecks out
on perilous seas; I know that I – faced
with such human turbulence – am runt and reckling,

am no commander nor able-bodied seaman to steer
the desperate into harbour. Knowing,
as I do, the lyric impulse touches on strange borders
and is entranced by mystery, affecting little.

REFUGEE

This, then, is the Christ.
They named him Alan, Alan Kurdi.
He is three years old.

Red T-shirt, short-sleeved;
navy-blue shorts, shoes navy-blue.
He has been washed ashore.

He lies, face down, on the wet shingles.
He is helpless; he has been helpless
all his life. He was obedient

in everything.
He was lifted aboard a crowded dinghy.
He had few words.

He is the word.
In him all things were created. And in him
all things hold together.

NOWHERE IN THE WORLD

I would send word, before I go into that
blank otherness, its silence and obscurity,
that I might hear King's College Choir sing to me

Allegri's *Miserere*; then, to cheer me, Barbara Hendricks
with Mozart's bright and vesper-sweet *Laudate Dominum*;
followed, because I have learned that it is so, by Vivaldi's

Nulla in mundo pax sincera. Finally, as they lay me down,
the Soggy Bottom Boys might choir: *I'm in the Jailhouse Now.*
When I have caught my breath in the New Land

I'll ask my Christ if I might spread my condor wings
and soar, soundlessly, through space and time to find –
April 13, seventeen forty-two, Dublin, Fishamble Street,

where I, amongst the gentry and the commoners, may fold
my wings and hear, its first time sung, *I know that my*
Redeemer liveth... and sense at last all yearning's done.

[Olivier Messiaen was captured by the German army in June 1940 and imprisoned in Stalag VIII-A, a prisoner-of-war camp in Görlitz, Germany. While in the camp, he wrote a short trio for three fellow-prisoners; this piece developed into the Quatuor pour la fin du temps: piano, violin, cello, clarinet – with Messiaen at the piano. The quartet was premiered at the camp, out in the rain, in January 1941.]

The composer wrote a Preface, telling how the Book of Revelation inspired him:

> Then I saw another mighty angel coming down from heaven. He was robed in a cloud, with a rainbow above his head; his face was like the sun, and his legs were like fiery pillars… He was holding a little scroll, which lay open in his hand. He planted his right foot on the sea and his left foot on the land… Then the angel I had seen standing on the sea and on the land raised his right hand to heaven. And he swore by him who lives for ever and ever, who created the heavens and all that is in them, the earth and all that is in it, and the sea and all that is in it, and said, "There will be no more time! But in the days when the seventh angel is about to sound his trumpet, the mystery of God will be accomplished, just as he announced to his servants the prophets."

I. *Liturgie de cristal*

Clarinet, blackbird, before dawn; trills and swoops, darkness through the treetops; somewhere the nightingale, trailing its violin skirts down slow steps to the lightening garden. The cello, repetitive, a bird's five-note melody, the piano, persistent, rhythmic, like the heartening pulse of the earth. Night-harmony. Somewhere, in the near-morning, a whiskey-glass pings in a glass-fronted cabinet. We are all falling off the earth into eternity. And the quartet: Nazis. Taliban. Boko Haram. Isis.

The Poem

I will have known the edgy festival of the poem, attempts
to touch hard truths of the immediate, and play a plausible

music, seeking what is beyond the facts and features, beyond
processes of was, and is, and will-be. To speak of the small

crack across the glass face of the carriage clock – meaning
a sorrow held in the long silence of an old country house.

*

Someday there will be the final lines; the last words
set down, completed, and incomplete. Poems, like leaves,

free to wander in breezes that take them, bearing their burdens,
their harvests. I will have prayed: Spare me Lord for my days

shatter like crystal; what is man that you should magnify him;
why do you tender towards him your heart of love? The light burns

dimly, fingers fidget on the sheets. Today I will lie down in dust,
and if tomorrow you come in search of me, I am no more.

II *Vocalise, pour l'Ange qui annonce la fin du Temps*

Piano. Angel like amalgam of exotic birds: the Lorikeet, the Quetzal, the resplendent Bird of Paradise, eclectic harmonies of otherwhere, the chutes of emerald downscales, the cataracts of incoherent calling, the tongue-tied response of the pianist. *Lento, lento currite...*

III *Abîme des oiseaux*

For solo clarinet. Owl-hoot. Night-birds' side-steps. Predawn arpeggios of outlandish night-fowl. The birds in their unseen bright colours are light in darkness. They are weariness in their silence. Night breathes out stars. Night breathes in stars. Night, breathless. Dawn returns with shadows, with a rainbow weeping. With light humming.

Dwellers in the Dust

Your dead shall live, their corpses shall rise: O dwellers in the dust,
awake and sing for joy – Isaiah
Many of those who sleep in the land of dust shall awake – Daniel

The house, neglected, has become an old
bachelor's disgrace; the decades have left detritus
in dank corners, a small cosmos of confusion,

cobwebs, grease and thrown rags, doors that will not
close, and a window cracked. In the greater cosmos
it may also be so, a mess of weeds and undergrowth,

the human form all stooped and grey, socks flung,
clothes unmeshed. And yet today, outside, cherry
blossoms, the blackthorn flowers are in riot,

the blue tits skittish about the dogwood and the clouds
grimly hastening westwards; already the daffodils
droop ragged, their green stalks streeling, the salleys

straighten after the squalls of winter. A man, not old,
is slipping slowly into foolishness; a girl, quietened,
holds two hands wonderingly over her swelling body

IV   Intermède

An interlude for the death of the piano, rebirth for violin, cello, and clarinet. Pizzicato days. The light, pizzicato. Darkness falling pizzicato. Ending of clarinet, and cello, and violin. The pianist: numb. Dumb. Head down, hands in lap, the glasses heavy. Scherzo ist das Leben, ist der Tod. Herr dieses Hauses!

V   Louange à l'Éternité de Jésus

Word. Lente, lentissimo. In principio. Pre-Genesis. Post-Apocalypse. Cello, its heart-song of the isolated one, soul, o soul, hold your breath, darkness is revealed, hold, breathe out, slow, soft, slow. World-soul. Time running. Out. The Death of Jesus reiterates cosmic evolution. Infiniment lent, extatique.

Last Things

The image haunts me: old-man father, and we
crowding the small room with our lives; he sits,
abstracted from us, hand raised to chin, and we
who have fallen shy of him, will not interrupt
the colloquy he is having with conclusions
reached over a long life.
                                        Crowding now to what
mercy in the end? To blot a name out of the book
of life?
            The mind's resources pitted for the last time
against the irregularities of the flesh, losses to be
negotiated, and the balanced, and balancing,
mounds of regret. After the long application of a life

to the grounds of on-going being, the spirit,
honing. Though dread still hovers.
Even beneath
faith. Is it then end, or beginning? Or perhaps
he is aware, merely, of the dimming light.

VI Danse de la fureur, pour les sept trompettes

The cosmos dances in unison. The underlying quaver beat of evolution is often augmented by a semiquaver, thus urging things forward. Gongs and trumpets, the six trumpets of the Apocalypse with their disasters … Vikings, Christians, Nazis, Taliban, Boko Haram, Isis… and the seventh, *tutti*, telling the end. The music of granite; the scringeing of steel, of boulders of violet anger, fortissimo, sheen on the belly of the cello, the black beast of the grand piano. These the instruments: use them, let the dancers jerk, automatons, the break-dance. Stop, then; take out the silken handkerchief, mop the brow. Be shark-race, be the scream, stagger, reach out…

VII Fouillis d'arcs-en-ciel, pour l'Ange qui annonce la fin du Temps

Have you seen rainbows cling in clusters? Have you heard the Angel announcing the end of time? The final rainbow, its colours are peace, wisdom, luminescence, consciousness, cosmogenesis, Christogenesis and notes sounding towards an Amen. Rise and fall, like rocking a baby, piano; cello, be mother; tremble, the world rocks to your fingers; you, the cosmic family, the hurried hush of evolution, the Christ-softness, the silence, the lava-birds, the cockatoo-stars, the silence inherent in rainbows, like blue-tit and blackbird and

redshank and greenfinch, for all of them are become angels,
taking wing, moving towards the finale, the Omega, the One,
the Was, the Is, the To-Be.

There shall be time no longer.

Turn the pages, softly as the falling of leaves.

Clouds were thunder-dark, crowding the sky;
all else was stillness, as if waiting;

the music-book has been closed. Words and music
fixed in the soil and memory. Enriching.

I heard a sudden
shrill cry, as of a child, articulate without meaning
above the brooding cityscape;

after the echo of the echo of the music, the particular
hour of trial has ended. Hearing the great harmony
of the one word: Amen. Standing faithful and
as witness, to the final end. And to the origins.

I thought a voice
beyond the darkness had learned the answer
to our mystery, and I looked up [–

Listen, the music said: I am standing at the door, knocking;
if you hear my voice and open the door, I will
come in to you and eat with you and you with me –]

five great birds

were circling, high above, climbing an invisible spiral
and drifting eastwards, towards the sea; buzzards,
alien birds, with one raw raven diving in at them.

Late evening now; applause has died away; even the shuffle
of the stunned has fallen still; the pale green horse and its
rider
have left the stage. Outside the sky appeared, like a scroll
unrolling, and all the islands shone in its light.

Where I stood, herons were mating high in the canopy
of an oak, shuddering the branches, shrieking the
commitment
to the being of heron, to the gawky and gaunt
elegant ugliness of their flight.

That you hang still, my Christ, clear-eyed in the storm
above me, and I stagger in the clutch of wet clay
that mires me. No tear will ever well up again in the eyes
nor congeal along a cheek, like blood, no finger will lift up
to rub against an eye.

Where we were aliens and pilgrims,
we are one now with the flow of the river, one
with the yellow eel at bay beneath the stones, one
with the kingfisher, and one in the gentle taking of hands
through the long, darkening night.

VIII Louange à l'Immortalité de Jésus

Duet. Couplets. Jesus, immortally dead on the cross. The Word finally made flesh. One word, simply, the word Love. Violin, tremolo; piano, pianissimo. Sheen on the body of the violin. A resurrection. Reaching the upper limits of the E string.

The transformation of earth into heaven: our dread is death, for it is the beginning of what we desire: fullness. In the inner universe Jesus lives forever. In us, the finite, the infinite. The mortal, the immortal. Worthless and immortal gold.

Let all the instruments fall still. Let there be a pause: breathless. Then let the applause begin for there will be joy untrammeled at the very end.

NAMING OF THE BONES

ALREADY A CHILD IS CRYING

Already a child is crying
when the galaxies exploded into being;

and a boy-child has been set afloat
– in a wicker-work basket of papyrus sedge –

down on the brown, swift-flowing Nile;
the beautiful widow Ruth, under the eyes of Boaz,

will be gleaning still along the fields of grain.
And a child, noon-time, is crying

while a family flees for refuge towards the sands of Egypt.
Almost midnight, moonmilk light

has been sliding over the upper-floor empty office desks
where a phone is intermittently ringing;

and already a child is crying, wrapped in cloths
and laid in a manger of wicker-work olive wood.

THAT CASTS NO SHADOW

Sunlight.   Almost noon.   Everything lies
at ease and unexpectant: as usual;   yet
different.   Grandmother, in her night-blue apron,
busy at sink and oven, is humming, timelessly:

as usual.   Lethargic cock-crow hour;   before
Angelus.   The girl is sitting by the half-open window,
quiet, almost doleful.   Not watching.   For days
no rain has fallen, what was green has been diminishing

to beige and even the lizards are stretched out listlessly.
Only the light gives word to the day,   means
anything.   Means nothing tangible, save the willingness

to accept whatever is.   Though she is startled
when the wings of the collared dove   that lifts
in a shadowless arc into the sky   suddenly applaud.

IN THE HILL COUNTRY

Old man, with liver-spotted skin, elder of the cloth,
no chick nor child, the incense of worship

teasing at your nostrils. Enriched from your dreams
of sanctuary, you found yourself near the borders from which

there is no turning back, for Israel fattens on its prisoners.
You are heavy with sadness at your years, though home

is a grove on a Pleasant Hill, fragrant with rose and jasmine,
orchids rising like orisons in the fields. You have served

long and well, lit the candles, moved with considered
ministrations, attended as witness at the altar's rim; expect

some validation. Though smitten dumb, allow mind and heart
to cede, to let the grace of suffering shape the torsions

of your will. The earth is gracious, name it so; love comes
in subtle guise, seize it now, in your liver-spotted hands.

THE BASELESS FABRIC

It has something to do with moonlight; he sleeps,
mild nights, without curtain or blind, and watches
down the shadowed corridors of the sky until he, too,
is shade. Along those same, spirited, darknesses

they come, the sibilances that word his dreams,
his fears: shibboleths, of course, and old boloney,
the light the moon casts being a shadow-ghost
of what is flesh; mouthings, too, cast up from depths

where truths he shirks from squirm, like eels sliming
among the weed-roots. He will wake and lean his brow
against the window, noting how the streetlights down below

gleam, like eyes, while police-cars, army trucks, come breathing
stealthily by, and sometimes an ambulance, its sapphire-blue
snaking siren screaming how we are vulnerable, and must flee.

ABIDING IN THE FIELDS...

To be ignorant is blessing, as a child is blessed
in its unknowing; better to yield to sun and wind,

to be stunned out of our wits – and to admit it –
by yowling storm and abrupt lightning, to be in awe

before the stars and their distinct music, to climb
into a tree to better look upon the earth; better to trust

to husbandry and offer out of poverty small gifts.
That night, one of the darkest, and brightest! sheep

shuffling and snuffling enough to bother us, yet all
I can remember is our stumbling over hump and lump

to touch upon the source. Sustenance proffered, out
of the rush of things that cause confusion, to some edge

where purpose might be glimpsed, and word shared. We left
poor gifts, feeling absolved of something, still unworthful.

HOT BLOOD

She holds him, Littlebody, wordless Honeybody now
who will howl and bring catastrophe. Two white doves
slaughtered, their hot blood sprinkled – why? since
blood-letting may not pacify divinity. Watchful old woman,

decades shrouded in black, all those blank yesterdays,
the stalled infinity. Around her the temple columns soar,
and all beneath is desiccated, gossip-whispers like dried
leaves slippered, a long hunger built into the walls. She tells

her beads, the sorrowful, her wrists and ankles swollen;
she has witnessed two world wars, a universe in traction,
and has withdrawn into glad, black-lace penumbra,

allowing that others will put the world, like a chaplet,
        together
again, to set it back on its way. Littlebody, perhaps? She will
fast, and pray – and yes! perhaps, the beads say, perhaps not…

LET THE CHILD PLAY

Because he, too, had dream-memories: of a time before time,
in the wild meadows of being, bright and hymning, of olive groves,
flamingos, of body non-

recalcitrant, of spirit lighter than air – but an age and ages without
companionship – and he sees in vision a boat in its tossing, scared
faces watching him;

remembers the breath-catching, tall mountain spaces, the honey
highland gentian, the commendation of the father, though down
in the troughs and hollows

he must confront the tears of a child in epileptic fits. Had his own
nightmares, too: the threatening spaces of Egypt; a thudding and
violent hammering;

his own face peering at him, distorted and bloodied, his mouth
open and unable to scream; body in revolt, spirit
deadened to stone.

Because now there is a golden haze floating on the buttercup meadow,
sunlight shining through the softest rain – and the lightning falls
in a flash of fire, down

out of the lifting sky, the sea, too, on fire, rulers of this world
tossed out like dung. Child, the mother said, don't be afraid, we
are here, we'll hold you.

OUTLAW

Because the story has not yet ended, because the world
is far from perfected – he withdraws to deserted places

to pray; he knows he has done such damage, scattered
seeds of dissent, shaken foundations, that he is outlaw;

knows, even in the deepest stillness, amongst
unspoiled orchids and the raw high cry of a hawk,

he is touched by the nearness of madness, by children
torn and tossed by demons: how can he soothe them, how

suffer them? Now we, we have old wells where we hang
rags of prayer on ash and hazel branch, where we circle

stiff as trees with longing. We have been given no manual
for the conduct of the heart, ours a persistence under duress,

spirits dulled by the ardor of abstinence, where our flustered
faith brings loneliness, and our quiet Lord seems absent.

FROM THE SCANDALOUS CHRONICLES

Goose-woman, ragged-haired and lone, in her scrawed,
half-tumbled cottage on the edge, her flock a white-feather
blizzard of coming-at-you scolding, and swallows
skimming the yard. Take no offense at this: a townland

not notorious, distant from the might of ocean,
from the hosting of shoppers across a mall, his footsteps
raising a small flurry of dust, nearing; footsteps
of the mourners, slower, nearing. They are come to entomb

her child, this somebody's only son; grief so great it is a silence,
swollen. But she, how she had cherished the unspoiled
whorls of his ears, the precise lunulae of his fingernails.

He stopped. They stopped. And – please don't cry – he said, as a lover
might say to his hurt love. Lifted the shroud, touched and handed back
the boy. Heart to heart; giving himself away; undoing the victory.

THE BREAD FROM HEAVEN

You stand, uncertain, by the juniper;
tall lilies are ghostly pale, there is a pre-dawn breeze;

spirt-presences, like the dewfall, gleam a moment
and are gone. I call to you, by name and nature,

catching at your elbow to turn you about.
I have been dead this while, this small eternal while

and have learned the dead are nourished – not
by spices, whiskies, sacred waters, but by your memories

of them. I have loved you, o love, before the flaring
of your being and now I crave that your stillness edge

towards mine. There are seeds of the blackberries caught
in my teeth, I yearn for a mouthful of spring. You

are still wandering the earth, and I am glad for Eucharist,
abundance, rock-rose and thorn, life like yours. Love.

Ring the doorbell; call out – God save all here. Shall you
eat today? shall you find shelter? Meek, he had said, and
humble of heart. But the hurt veteran, stretched in a heap
on cardboard packaging, its rough edge rucked with wet,

lacks dignity and freedom. Seditious, to turn us from the starry
heavens, to the tar-spattered verges of our roads! Remember
the angels – Herbert, Hopkins, de Chardin – who emerged,
shimmering like a mirage and took shade beneath the terebinth;

remember the young woman, standing shaven-headed at the corner
whose dirt-caked asking hand I refused, who smiled at me
and nodded, so I felt justified. But came back later to offer her one

twenty-euro note, which she generously accepted. I saw Christ-Fox,
on the damp, empty street under sickly light, his profane
half-sideways lope, his crusty irruption into our urban gardens.

NO OFFENCE INTENDED

The up-shaft, re-used, is in position, last week's blood caulking it.
The criminal, slathered already in blood and sweat,
labours under the crossbeam's weight, and all the scourging;
then thuck of hammers, big-headed nails driven through wrists

into the riven beam. You must not take offense at him, he
is not the guilty one. Ropes heist beam and body, jolt-drop them
into place. Children, at play by the city wall, look up to watch.
The light is fierce, the heat incensed. Square-headed nails

are driven in each side the shaft, through the ankle-bones;
unquenchable fire in wrists, ankles, chest as he rides the nails,
gasps for breath. T, for Tau, for trauma, torture, for the love

greater than which… There is no comforting; he has taken
our depth of hurt and degradation. The outlaw Christ.
Take no offense at him. Love's fault. And let the children play.

NAMING OF THE BONES

London, June 2017

I looked up and saw you, your distorted body
writhing again in agony. There is a season, the Big Book says,

a time to die, a time to weep, and a time for peace;
no one, it says, can understand what is happening under the sun.

I saw the bare breast heaving, that once beautiful breast;
I hurt for you, for your beloved once beautiful, body, each twist or twitch,

each reach and wrench adds to the fire in your flesh
and bones. I plead to creator lover God for you, to ease your pain,

to mother you. I wince once more at the bitter-spittle angers
of humankind: the blunted iron nails driven through your caring hands,

your tender feet; so that impossible you hang from them,
and stand on them; the muscles cramp and spasm, and your face,

so beautiful once, is contorted with spit and ugliness, with
blood and sweat and tears. Today, my Christ, June 14, twenty-seventeen,

Grenfell Tower in London was engulfed in flames; inestimable
furnace, suffering unbearable. A child appears for a moment, at a window

of the sixteenth floor, a moment only, frantic, waving:
to a not-there-saviour; you? We hurt, my Christ, we hurt. Why is our spittle

hot with bitterness? Words, the Big Book says, can be
wearisome, a chasing after wind. And yet… the world breaks. The world

re-forms. But the beautiful body breaks, and yields.
Yearning and grief trouble us. At the heart of it. You. Hurting.

It was early. A dawn wind
bringing its chill. There was hazy light, then a little more.

The stillness of white lilies, drooped, and a garden in dawnlight.
No murmur of thunder. Yet the whole cosmos must have drawn itself

together, and shuddered.

[I was driving south, to Monaco; it was Saturday, and an Easter snow fell softly. I stopped, to visit Reims Cathedral. I found a dim and vaulted emptiness and chill but stood entranced before the blue in Chagall's stained-glass windows, Christ's death and resurrection. It is a dark blue radiant with light, and I drove on, warmed by that blue, my heart singing. Evening, somewhere beyond Chalon sur Saône, I found a small auberge; I dined: charcuterie and fromage, tarte au citron, a half-bottle of good Burgundy wine. Cointreau. (To live within the limits of the expected, I thought, is not to be alive). I slept like a holy man and came awake next morning, in the faintest light, hearing the hiss of traffic out on the motorway, knowing happiness, well-being, and direction. Outside, that grey mist lifting, I watched a swan go slatternly over the surface of a lake, ungainly, straining till its lift of power showed that something marvellous had been achieved; it rose like a white-fleece relict of winter, bringing light and warmth into the morning. I set out again, south, along the motorway.]

Can the whole earth hold its breath?
And time, can it pause? We ask, knowing there is no such thing

as time. World is so wonderful it shocks beyond belief. The woman,
turning, slowed by grief, could scarcely see through the half-light;

trees stood, like sentries at the borders of darkness; the chill
persisting. A shape, as of a man, perhaps a gardener, startled her

and she reached for reassurance.

[The common-or-ditch old sparrow bathed in the dust; the beloved's face had faded within a mist of days. She came, hauling the drag-down burden of self, through the rusty squall of a gate, along a pathway scrunching under her tread. In a corner, dark-blue bell-flowers wanted to ring. It was barely dawn but a young man was sitting there, dressed in white. Swanlike. She felt, she did not hear, the words. The very earth breathed light; she heard the trees in their protective loving whisper secret. This, the very core of the universe. As if the impossible wonderful was simply natural. She understood, all at once; moment when the magnificence of it fell apparent, she, struck open, emptied, taut in expectation. She was cell of creation's well-being, her name spoken out with love, all yesterdays held in pollen, in star-speck, spore and tomb-dust.]

She reached for reassurance. Her name was spoken, with that
old love she had come to live for. Her life became song:
What happened, happened once only, never before, never since.
Even lightning may strike the same tree twice. But this, just once.

LIKE THE DEWFALL

A BOY-CHILD

Amen of Creation

There is a boy, urging a child-sized US army jeep
around a dew-damp Achill Island yard,
pedalling and steering, and the small stones bump
the khaki-green, star-marked plaything;

a cockerel scolds loudly as he cock-steps along the wall,
battle and stand-off
between cockerel and boy being everyday events
of moment. Distant, familiar and unfamiliar, that child,

there where the pine-tree grove was bounded
by flowering escallonia bushes, where robin,
thrush and blackbird sang, where the Angelus bell
told over the Incarnation. Noon, he is in the parlour,

at the piano, much against his will: battling the scales,
the fingering, the sharps, the flats…
Tempo! time! time! the music-mother calls;
on the lacquered lid the tick-tock-tick of the metronome,

while the world turns outside and the fuchsia is in bloom.
Adagio, cantabile, softly, softly;
from this time out it will all be *crescendo, allegretto* – and yet!
amen to the music, and amen to the universe,

– from cockerel to hump-back whale, from quark to galaxy –
amen to the Christ-child, chortling in the crib, new-earthed
heart of creation, who is, who was, who is coming-to-be;
to sustained harmony of the spheres: amen! *Pianissimo*. Begin.

*

They said that the stork had flown, late,
    through the night sky, in over Bunnacurry; but he

was approaching the age of reason and knew it had to be
    Big Seán heron, scrawny-bodied and heavy-winged,

creaking his wagon-self back to the bog-pools and
    water-lily ponds of the lower mountain. In school,

the Brothers harped always on the fall, loading on fresh minds
    the burdens of original sin and guilt, as if they –

young-lads in short trousers and fraying ganzies –
    had been mitching in the garden when the ancestors

bit into fruit that left chalk-dust forever in the mouth.
    They fought, as boys will fight – bloody noses, purpled eyes –

and they raided the smaller orchards of the island, though
    sensing there were deeper purposes, and they'd learn them.

*

Bog-boy, they called him, for his dreaming
among the cuttings; he was at home

up on the turf-bank, down in the cutaway,
moorland breathing in its variegated and sepia

ease. He loved the world-berating
sweet-bird wheatear, the sudden snipe,

soprano trilling of the skylark; loved
the dragonflies, their wings, those forms

of a polychrome antiquity. He tip-toed over
the daffodil innocence of bog-asphodel, fingered

the white-fluff stuff of bog-cotton tufts, embraced
the lean-to wigwam footings, the turf-sods

wet with the life-sap of earth, and rain, and timelessness.
His delight, to be barefoot for a while,

squishing the ooze of mud between his toes, hearing
the distant haling sounds of the ocean. Knowing himself

in sunshine, to be one with the life of the peat-bog,
had come upon him insidiously as the dewfall,

and in dusk-light, under a peach-soft moon
with stars bright against bright on the blue-grey

mantle of the sky, he sensed himself to be
cell of the cosmos, fleck on the foam of the flux.

*

To each beginning its new ignorance, a world
to know, a shore to step out from. Discovering
once more, before night turns full dark, how light
has shifted from clouded blue and how the heart

is worrying again at the impossible mystery, each of us
being a mere creature, of history, of the variable, on-going
flow. The road out of Bunnacurry back towards Keel
holds its own importance; critical, too, are the steps

down from the pier to the mud-flats when the tide is out;
like ribs of the unearthed dinosaur, the black
timbers and spars of the trawler that has been sinking

year by year into the digesting belly of estuary while clear
water from the mountain spring darkens under turf-banks
and meets and merges with the salt arteries of ocean.

*

He was drawn by the sounds of small streams in flood after rain;

eels, over the stones, eased past; honey-coloured trout, little-bodied,
beautiful and supple, fair-flecked, held themselves, mouths
gulping, steady against the downflow;

the joy of shaping a flesh-saucer with two hands to drink, supping
like a stag or mistle-thrush;

fishing in the deeper pools, watching a cork jig-jogging, catching
mostly nothing (and pleased at that), but holding the delight
forever;

the moment, kneeling, gazing down into the purest water, hearing
the Angelus bell ring its insistent message from the monastery,
turning to look up and querying – *angelus?* thinking what
an angel might be,

till the wet and cold against his knees told him again of flesh.

Knowing later, when smitten at last with the Christ, he had been always
turning, unconsciously, to face him, flinching already
from the embrace.

*

It begins, too, with a slight
fingernail-pittering against the panes,
that spittle-spatter knocking
of the smallest hailstones
out of the largest sky;

he will press his face to the window,
in delight; the world, skirt-gathering
against all things standing,
will relish its dance of grey-dark
light across the fields.

Ebullience, creation says,
is of the essence, fecundity
from vacuity towards wholeness.
The greenfinch comes, little quantum
of luminous greens, beak feverish

at the feeder; cosmogenesis is the word
– a few seeds scattered by its hunger
onto snow-softened ground. The sun,
emerging, will cast a wet
shivering along the verges

and a truck, passing, will make
a loving, hissing sound. Knowing
the beating of the heart of matter,
resplendence out of centre into centre,
he will be vigilant, and fused.

*

Come stand awhile, here, at the outermost edge
of the world, the end and the beginning;

Ireland, Atlantic weathers, the cliff face sheened
with rain; sunlight glints off the schist diamonds,

a dusty dribble of stones splitters down into the sea.
Here the child knelt, on the window-seat, gazing out

at hard, inhibiting elements; on the upstairs landing,
in a cut-glass vase, Delft-blue and linen-white hydrangeas

stood in autumnal light; he could hear grandmother,
who dressed in black, sobbing behind her bedroom door.

The child was learning that there are stations of sadness
on the long journey, from *introibo* towards *amen*, because,

she told him, years of dreams appeared to her, this late,
to roost like bats from branches of diseased elms. Stand,

this precious moment, on the bridge at Achill Sound; watch
all the oceans of the world come teeming out of Blacksod Bay

to roar and crush through the gullet of the Sound;
at high tide there will come quiet, a still point, before the turn,

when all the oceans of the world come thrashing back
as if all cosmic being must depend upon it. His, then,

is the music of island. But sometimes there is another music,
in the great hall, that moves him; two dressed in black are seated,

edged, on black piano stools; there is a background
of indeterminate cloth, grey-black; the auditorium stilled,

a few small lights mark exit; two grand pianos are standing
poised, great wings spread. This will be Messiaen, *Visions*

of Amen, each piano challenging the other, each holding
to cliff and crossing, the beginning, and the end. Taut

understanding for the child, like walking barefoot over
bulwark stones, winds crying, while out at sea the whitest

gannets dive; on the strand, he can hear the calls
of oystercatchers, their black and white, their blood-red dagger-bills.

*

Times he played, at a neighbour's sorrow-house,
out in the backyard where hens –
Rhode Island Red and Leghorns – stepped
in slow and skirty busyness

across the hen-shit-spattered ground,
close to the black lake of the sweet-singing birds. No
loveliness to the place, merely
stories of a father who left for easier fallows and did not

return. The sons
fought with stony fists to dim the shame in their own eyes,
the daughter sat in listlessness,
watching the dog – dirt clotted through his hairs –

scratch at himself with fury. Always
the fox, and the dawnlight scattering of feathers,
while the mongrel stretched in the ashes, and a light
shone beneath the picture of a fading Sacred Heart.

Noon and the boys' frayed shirts
were hand-scrubbed and hung over a thorn bush
to dry. Hen-woman made small money
selling eggs and tending graves,

watched the bus each evening and kept the table set:
plate and cup and saucer sporting
a painted house and the word *home* inscribed in blue,
with egg-cup and tarnished pewter apostle spoon.

THE MONASTERY

Amen of the Stars and Planets

The road across the island has been widened;
late in the year the holiday caravans, the campers,

will have drifted home. If you pass this way, pause
at the turn by the new school; find a mild mid-morning

offering merely mistings of rain. Draw your car in
where the gateway pillars have long been overgrown

with trailing shrubbery; you will find a new,
though rickety gate opening on a laneway. Bring

quiet in your heart. Close the gate carefully against the world
and walk. Perhaps you, too, are searching for fount

and fostering, have learned that they drift away
like the many-rainbowed bubbles of your childhood days.

*

You stand now
on an island upon an island where you may find again
you are not an integer, unit among units, here you may
lose yourself in richer being,

new-world-old,
rediscover wholeness and a purpose to your days. Start
down the sandy, stony lane, watching for mud and puddles.
The rhododendron bushes

form wild patternless curtains
on either hand; a breeze brushes the leaves that glisten still
with this morning's dewfall. Come to the smaller gate,
halfway along,

where the boy
entered the two-room school that was and is not.
Where he suffered the boyish challenges at real or wished-for
injuries, wet finger touched to the cheek,

like a glove flung down
at the feet of nobility; wars have always been part of it,
the bully ignorant but counting on his fists. Always,
the extravagance

of the rhododendron blooms,
the dark and sprawling branches and the earth
littered with petals, stirred something in him, a sense
of remotest loss, an emptiness

compounded
with a joyfilled wonder. He, young anchorite, musing
in the dim light that fell through leaf and branch, was
for long, delicious moments,

at peace
with the instances of body. Creation was part of it
and it, all of it, was part of him; being, and being there,
sufficient, it was fullness, it was world.

*

The sun shines on playing fields where seagulls
bicker over crumbs; the window is a little dusty
and tantalising in its height; the walls are rich

with charts of a pastel simplicity, and one big-faced
clock, portentous, swings its pendulum, slowly, too
slowly. Boys tough and fragile, practising swagger,

hold faith with complex workings of the adult
catechisms and stored economies. He learned
that words could grow, long-stemmed and flourishing,

from the ends of his fingers and form patterns
on a white field. Today it is ruin, roofless,
gable-ends crumbling, stone gnawed and blackening,

briars burgeoning where a door should be, and only
the persecuting winds come crowding through
the tumbled walls and rubble. Barbed wire will hold you

back from the mess of muck and sploshes, the starved
grass, thistles, the rushes. He will be standing there
for ever, at that margin, watching out, staring in.

*

He was sent to the monastery, late in the day, for milk;
a half-mile of open road, between deep ditches;

it was, in the late seasons, miserere time, a nervous rush
down the dark lane to the lit side-window where

Brother Cassius filled up the can. Fear of the Lord,
they said, is the beginning of wisdom, that Lord

who numbered all the stars and had assigned them names.
Fear now was darkness, terror and dismay, the world

black, like the raven and her young, cackling. His mind
crackled with images, the *danse sauvage* of Mars and Mercury

and Pluto over the blacked-out ballroom floor of space:
madmen, werewolves, devils and Cloven-Hoof himself

reaching for him... and he prayed to the God who holds
the oceans within bounds, who feeds the young of ravens

when they cry out in their nests... He ran, marking
tempo, élan and repos, rise and fall, air and road,

a drum-beat heart-beat between the intervals of silence.

*

Once, in the guest parlour of the monastery, two
grand pianos, winged and elegant, like seraphim;
on the pastel-coloured walls, stylized pictures:
Francis of Assisi and Anthony of Padua, lives
dedicated to their this-world other-world Christ.
Under shaky spotlights, the pianists; in the shadows
the guests, bemused, in feast day best, and smitten.
Mild applause. The pianists bow and settle. Two
fussed page-turners, the music of Messiaen furious
as thunder-burst, the harmony and counter-harmony
of creation, comet-falls of chords, chromatics, scales,
fingers and wrists of the priest-like bodies of the pianists
pre-occupied by sacrament. The guests all sitting, strained,

half-stifled coughs, a little self-conscious shuffling,
while above it all, in the night air, the monastery bell
waits silent, poised and ponderous in its louvered tower.

*

You must move on, there are further gates to open.
At lane's end you will find relicts of greater trees,
elms, oaks… ragged as scarecrows. To your right,

arthritic remains of an orchard, straggle apple-trees
with bunched fists of fruit, yellowing and bitter,
weeds rampant and cluttering around the roots.

Among fallen stones, seek out echoes of the soul-full
prayers; sparrow and robin watch you, singing hymns
that have not wavered. Pass on, by the hollowed-out

windowless dairy, the collapsed sheds of the farm,
green-washed walls and bleak, derelict buildings, beams
hanging. There will be sheep-droppings everywhere

in the monastery parlour, where lamps went out long ago
and the warm light fell away, into deep time. The monks,
in brown habits, chanting the *Lumen Christi*, conducted

cosmic stirrings across the island; but theirs was a God
immutable and chastening, their world a garden, fallen
to weed and weevil, because of sin inherited. The parlour,

where whiskey was generously poured, where prayers
were weighty and vows preserved, has long been floorless
and only sheep find shelter against the cloister walls.

*

Turn now, to find the cemetery, with its small
coterie of saints. The plaque says Welcome,
Sister Death. There is peace, and silence, ocean
distantly breathing, breezes sighing absence;

you may find yourself suddenly whelmed
to know how you love this earth, where the Christ
is flesh, and part of it, how people everywhere
are quickening beautiful as light. Radiance comes

from star and planet, the bracing sky is brightening.
Do not say they failed; simply, the precise need
ended. Jesus, awkwardly taken from the cross,

was not a failure. You are on the verge of prayer,
conscious again of our world's grace, aware
of hurrying time, of who you are, and when, and where.

THE FURIES

Amen of the Agony

Atlantic Ocean comes sweeping in
with violence round the black rocks,
the waters restive, frantic, passionate;

near shore the 'Great Rock'; further out
'West Great Rock'; and then – the 'Daisies' –
submerged, risen, submerged; chaotic with foam

(white, like the flowers) from crashing waves; energy
of cosmic force, the source that urges
all creation onwards, outwards, towards

the close, omega, the Pleroma.
All flesh is flayed by storm, soul is swallowed
in vastness and spat out; bleak is it, times,

as the sodden yellow-ochre acres of bogland
eking themselves out from road to distant hills. Then
the 'dásachtaí', the daisy rocks, the furies –

breaching sometimes, more often known
only by the feverish whitewaters round them;
that have drawn currach and trawler to them,

smashed timbers, brasses, iron into sad debris.
Erinyes, the underworld; soul fraught and
bewildered, finds yet a still point, Christ-wise,

in the chaos of being; the soothing of spirit,
a white sail distant and holding, islands of the sea
glistering in haze on the furthest horizon.

*

From Purteen pier he watched
a tick-tack half-deck trawler slowly
enter the harbour, black smoke roping behind it,
and the cluttered deck dangerous with coil and cord –

back from sea-slaughter, mackerel
cut in half for bait and dumped into a bucket
while up above the seagulls swooped and screamed.
The crew, yellow-bright rubber aprons smeared with blood,

tossing and pitching the catch onto the pier:
blue, the requiem shark, its armoured back, the off-white
flop of its belly, its strike out of darkness, to the kill; conger,
hooped perfection stiffened in the ugliness of death; monkfish,

mud-coloured, freaky, frog-fish and sea-devil,
squatina squatina, sea-bed walker and lurker; splatted
on the pier edge. Fish-boxes, too, sea-flesh, sea-food, ripe.
The vast wreckage of the basking shark, humbled and hauled

up the slipway greased by its blood, to be hacked
and sawn into shivering heaps of blubber. A gentle
monster, jaws gawping open like a barn door. Octopus.
Unlike the watcher, evolution not yet conscious of itself.

*

Behind high walls and a garrisoned gate
full-grown trees, and walking figures, not walking,
merely slow motion, forwards, backwards, willing to meld

with air, to find themselves at rest again,
underground, or tableted to relative oblivion.
Big House hush of grand pianos and black-suited

quartets; no parlour rooms, dim cells only,
with one-way peep-hole, to watch from this world
into a next. Minds strayed, as if out on the bewildering sea,

water-walking over the deeps, the slaughter,
the wrecks, and high above, the stars, rock-dead
in the great vast. Shadows among the olive trees. Demons

cackling in the mind. The pendulum ticks
and tocks, each tick a century, each tock… Like
Ishmael, is he, on the ocean; Yeshua, is he, in the garden;

Legion: floundering among the fluid makings
of the universe. At night sometimes, the inmates
keep a weather eye open, to plead the inscrutable tides

of God, this side of death. Anchored to human
frailty, what can they do but count the bubbles lifting
to the surface and blossoming into air. When we go out

of the demesne of time, this question: what of the broken mind?

*

Light fading; edge of the pounding
Atlantic Ocean; sting of salt on the air; curlews –
challenged congregations scattered
along the shore – lift

strangely musical burble-calls. Herons are mating
high in the canopy of a larch,
shrieking their commitment
to the blessedness of heron, to the gaunt

and elegant ugliness
of their flight. We are, with the crying birds, turf
of the turf, spirit-particle
of the bewildering God. We groan inwardly, leave

illuminated handscripts,
like flowerheads of bog cotton. Picture the man
on his knees in an olive garden;
(the distress oh Christ, my Christ!) cries like notes

played in the high register of the black pianos,
like bird-calls, lapwing, kittiwake. At times the music
seems to be neither of this world
nor the next; there are

silences, attending on the messenger angel. The Word,
taking human flesh out of a too-great love,
found himself ground down
– at the shifting-shingle edge of being –

under the clear incomprehension of his adopted kind
and flung on the shores of suffering.

*

There was a young boy, introvert, involved, grown expert
at the pleasures of isolation, in love with tree-top

and sea-pool, familiar with hawk and yellowhammer,
expert too with the long tapers and Latin responses

– *Kyrie, Requiem, Sanctus* – pattering about the sanctuary
in altar-slippers, preparing for the black-habited and

dismal rituals. Bearing him slowly to consciousness
of human anguish, and of loss. He will ring, as usual,

the bells at sacrament, shut the gilt-bound, delicate pages
of the big book carefully, but tears and keening for the children

burnt to death in Ballymoney will colour the season
sable, will leave his young yet unscathed life exposed, as if

dew-scales had fallen from a perfectly-formed
green leaf and left it bared to a chafing sun.

CARILLON AND BELLS

Amen of Desire

Something stubborn about the call and urge,
how the young man lay in his cramped seminary room
as he watched the progress of the stars across
the night, knowing the world outside is rock

and difficult, sensing the goodness of his body
and its demands, fearing that God was circling him
at a distance like a white-wolf pack at the far
edges of the pines. Soon the bell would ring,

sharply, at the lip of dawn for matins and mental
prayer, with distances ahead for spirit both
and body. Mind, as ever, unquiet, heart swelling

towards a life's willed-for abundance, a love
both delicate and strong, wolf heart, and lamb's,
God longed for, sought through the dark woods.

*

Noontime he had sung, with others,
(like a flock of sea-birds on the shore, facing
into the winds) Palestrina: *sicut cervus desiderat*...Mid-

afternoon, in the conservatory – a great, inverted
glass bowl, with beams of cedar, with bougainvillea,
the Silk Road giant lily – the words and music haunted,

"like the deer my soul thirsts for you, oh Lord", as if it were
the Magdalen, tip-toeing towards the tomb. *Sehnsucht*;
yearning, *desiderium*… Dressed in black soutane and cincture

and still young, question of will, and constancy,
question, too, of profound reservations. Late afternoon
he climbed to the dusty music-room in the seminary attic

to practise on the old upright piano: Liszt's
Liebestraum, but it was all false notes and butter-fingers,
all inconsistency. Late evening, the sky was a rich patterning

of saffron light and a full moon lounged at rest
behind threads of cloud, while the incomprehensible
heavens were punctured by faint stars. The city skyline fell away

in darkness; he watched that foresting of lights,
and thought of all who would lie, like him, that night,
unquiet, the ache in the heart uneased, the thirst unquenched.

*

Under the dust-heavy alders and the briars, here
where the city trams go past with a great hiss,
tilts a small, half-hidden one-person tent, dark blue,
with trash and cans around, a foetid smell, a nobody

living rough. Not far the ever-present invitation
of the canal. One God-chastened, God-cherished
soul has come to this. Late-day winds are ferrying
rain across the trees; traffic wheezes, urgent for home,

carrying through the city the vehemence of a new
millennium. Faint light appears, sickly, through
the plastic of the tent. Perhaps here the Christ
will dine tonight, or call a friend to him in the hours

before dawn. Earth spins; here is a soul flung
into elliptical orbit around the sun, human mechanisms
coming undone at the welds, the rivets, the soldering;
as if God Yahweh had drifted out into darkspace.

*

I was driving home when I spotted it: the snipe –
bog-bleater, she-goat of the air –
this small-bang explosion
out of the aftergrass that will rocket away,
low over the wetlands and the bottoms, that
disappears through a hole in the glowering sky,
now caught, this winter dusk, in the car's headlights,
so out-of-place and present it shocked
and delighted, this old evolution's
almost-perfect bird-body,
this mistress of flight, this
querulous miracle of the countryside.
Comes, I thought, from somewhere
beyond the ditch, some local, cosmic source, hides
over the rainbow, beyond human fumbling.

*

Snow has been falling through the darkness,
the night sky blotted out, with its innumerable

stars and galaxies; tomorrow
the fields and hedgerows will be lit

by a generous blanketing of white. Annual
the marvel of it, the shortwhile

loveliness and wonder. Even more wonderful
the miracle: that already

before the Word that set the marvel of creation
in evolving motion – over 13 billion years, imagine! –

you and I, in our souls and bodies, were destined
to be together in the miracle of love, for this

short, this irreplaceable, lifetime. We, as one,
being more than selves, we are earthed, part

of the full moon risen high over the red gate, part
of the young hare, unafraid, settled

among the fading rudbeckia, sharing
these years, the darkness and light, the grief, the gladness.

for Ursula

*

It was a long day of spittling rain; the ugly
old-brown walls of the hospital
appeared to sweat; a little chatter in the corridors,
the waiting-rooms crowded, one small boy irritatingly

tock-tocked his foot against a chair-leg. A neon light,
on in the grey-bleak afternoon, was flickering; couples
sitting apart together, murmuring, watching the clock.
I whispered to myself: Oh Christ, my Christ.

But we were given glimpses into the being of cosmos –
the sonogram: black and white and greyscale,
placenta, the baby – the amniotic sea, the spirit
moving over the waters, offending chaos; it was

a shumbling vision, beautiful and awful, the heartbeat,
chest, neck, the umbilical cord… moment to cherish,
to hold faith, bells ringing deep in the heart, carillon, love;
and the decisions, there since the Big Bang, locus earth,

place Dublin, time the twenty-first century, year of the Lord.
I prayed to honour them, the ancestors in their pale awayness,
and our own impatiently waiting generations. A hint
of a soft-flesh, soft-bone, stirring contradiction

to nihilism, like Vincent's painting of *Almost Blossom* in San Rémy,
or Czeslaw Milosz's 'one real droplet of dew'. This day
we coasted with the guiding angels, with saints and birdsong
of galaxy and star. I whispered to myself: Oh Christ, my Christ.

THE HOME PLACE

Amen of Birdsong, of the Saints and Angels

Cattistock, in Dorset; go through the kissing-gate and make
your way onto the public footpath; there will be sheep and you
will feel for them, their matter, the hard bone of their hooves,
the stone that is stuff of their brains.

Through the next iron gate, its high squeal, low groan, and in the
wet hollow between trees the holy well, in dark shadow, trickles
slowly, its waters disappearing in source and destination.

A robin, solitary, watches you from the alders, its song as old as
psalm and chronicle.

Twilight is grey, slightly misty.

The churchyard with its leaning bockety gravestones holds its
humps of grass in quietness; the church itself, stout in buttress
and stone-angled presence,
stands doleful, watchword and reassurance.

There is a wooden gate into the village; the latch sticks a little;
the one long street is deserted under off-yellow light.

Hesitantly you enter the "Fox and Hounds"; all heads turn,
in sudden silence, until you find a corner, under black beams,
sit in relief and wait. Here you would draw a curtain against
all difference, remembering that solitary boy who knelt, years
gone, on a window-seat, face against cold glass, gazing out onto
improbable imaginings.

What purpose the unweaving and unravelling, if not for the sake
of marvel, what purpose the searching all without, since you hold
within you the Christ, closer to you than the stirrings of your heart?

Now you share with the one you love a sweet Dorset cider, with hill
lamb and champ and Dorset apple cake.

You are content.

Too soon it is dark outside, time to amble back.

There is rain, a soft wind bustling wet against you, together you are
hastening
back through the churchyard and along the path; a sheep, eyes wide
with fright, leaps away from human presence into the thickening
night.

*

Saints and angels, of all feathers, pass at will
between time and timelessness; like birds, they
have their languages and only God can comprehend them all;

the words I write – although recalcitrant –
come shyly out of multitudes, they seek to clarify, and they
– in their unruly way – attempt to prophesy, for they are placed

between there and here, between then
and now, to signify the end-in-view, Omega, the Christ.
Birdsong and birds, the choiring of saints and angels, rehearse

that purity I strain for, as Messaien worked
to vocalise the blackbirds, larks and nightingales, the sounds
he discovered in the veins of the meadows, in the forest's bones –

bird-notes, marshland chords, calls, trills, croaks,
the hard-ground treading of saints and the Ariel hastening
of angels, though, having suffered the tuneless hearts of Nazi camps

he knew that even the most tender music breasts
against the edging of death, and therefore translated his songs
into the hammers, wires and ivories of two raven-black grand pianos.

*

The past is a scattering of barnacled rocks
        at the edge of ocean; indoors we keep
journals of sorrows and accidents, though
        most wonderful has been the ongoing
common everyday, too easily forgotten:
        letters cut into the gravestone, merge
with the stone. Back door, its ditch-dark green,
        rain-swollen, scraping open or scraping shut
has scored a perfectly-shaped quarter-circle
        on the black flags and gouged a large splinter
out of itself at the base where a field-mouse
        might whisper through. One nightfall, Christmas
Eve – before electricity had driven angels and all
        supernaturals off the island, when oil-lamps
still stood elegant, like women in a painting
        by Toulouse-Lautrec – father took me out
into the heathlands, the hill lit only by a weak
        starlight; then turned me round to see:
in all the windows of the houses, there were
        candles lighting, their intimacy and presence

transfiguring the world. I stood, awed and,
        somehow, triumphant. No lights have ever since

been adequate, to the birth, to the remembrance.

*

[from "A Leitrim Townland", by Ursula Foran: Leitrim Guardian, 2018]

"It is hard to imagine that, before the ravaging of their potato crop, upwards of seventy people lived here. It is also hard to imagine that, even further back, these fields and rocks echoed to the tones of the Irish language for far longer than to the English we now speak here."

These are the fields of Leitrim, and here
the wild meadow, grasses, with celandine, meadowsweet
and maidenhair…
Apple trees down by the red gate, a chestnut tree

from Herbert's Leighton Bromswold, an oak –
thriving – from an acorn Heaney gathered by Thoreau's
Walden Pond.
In the wet-daub earth is the dwelling-place of our unruly God;

birdsong perfected, even jackdaw, heron, water-hen,
the very shrieks of hooded crow and magpie, those street-cleaners
and working angels
of an evolving world. Ancestors, in the lenient light of eternity,

hover here; wonder holds itself against us, for we are
finite insects grasping for infinity. It is cosmos, the spirit
coming down like dewfall,
and onerous our tasks of care. Soon the wild meadow

will renew itself, in season, accommodating deaths
and rebirths; familiar world, beautifully unfamiliar, enriched,
enriching,
with, sometimes, the scarlet call of a poppy.

*

The portal through which you have entered this world
is not the one through which you will exit. In Bunnacurry,

gravemounds shuffle over against one another
while ghostly mists relentlessly pass across, water dreeps

from stone crosses, from fuchsia where robin and wren
fall silent; a heron stands firm as an effigy near a ditch;

even the keeper of the graves has gone to ground,
the rusting gate has a rusting lock. Grandfather lies

in a grave too large for him, saxifrage and lungwort
cover him, and small white-stone chippings. This world

enclosed, is a garden, perishable and bewildering; holds
the quiet of a Vermeer interior, the sure-footed steps

of a Bach partita. What is it, then, that has flung you
off your horse into the dust and blinded you with light?

Gather yourself off the ground; there is one who is; seek
him out, present yourself at his door; he asks only your love.

*

He who sets the aurora in the clouds is enamoured
of human, earth and cosmos; for what would he be
without song-birds? without saints and angels?

enamoured, too, of the billions of insects daily sucked
into the radiators of long-distance trucks come crossing
the careening world: signals of the broken Christ;

(and where have they taken him, my courteous Lord?)
There is, too, the improbable colouring of parakeets,
the notion of time, the imponderable size of the universe.

Unbelievable the human spine with its curves and vertebrae
in under the skin as Himalayas and Karakorum are snuggled
in under snow; and the rainbow, its spectrum, stretching

from heart to heart, from Achill Island to the Antarctic.
It is heavy-duty soil out there, beyond and beyond, with
lavish mansions of the blessed dead; the children of light –

guiding angels of the galaxies – are shoaling in their billions
beyond our ken, the first frontier being flesh, the second,
clay. I am in body, bodily, on this island, earthed. I know

the world to be a living thing, a heart beating in every tree,
everything in motion, call it love, the agape of rock
and marigold, and the eros of a selfless sympathy.

*

I came back to my place in the pew, self-conscious
as always, and knelt to savour, as always,

the bread, unleavened. Hard November sunlight
scarce touched the early chill, and the windows

were colouring the day: emerald, blood-red
and Virgin blue. I could sense around me

the earthly living, and at my back the dead; waves
of refugees fell and rose within me, the children,

orphaned and at sea. It was a hosting, then and there,
heart calling to heart, squalls across the galaxies,

the chalice, embossed and silver-wrought, lifted
into the air in spate. I could hear, for a moment,

the music of oneness, and like Beethoven's 9th
creation played its symphony with all the instruments

and the cosmic voices in full harmony. I bowed my head
and closed my eyes. And then there were only –

candles lit before the November list of names
of the dead, the sounds of a small-town congregation

shuffling back to the pews, and clouds outside
bringing the chancel back, as always, into gloom.

POINT OF PURE TRUTH

Amen of Judgement

Around the baptismal font, *point vierge*, back
of the church, they are standing – grandfather,
still sprightly, grandmother, not yet slowed in flesh;
their daughter, weak after the birthing, but radiant;

son-in-law, upright and brimming-over father;
godmother, early twenties, tuberculosis; godfather,
wooing her in hopelessness; the baby, unaware
and snuffling; the celebrant, with the oils and words.

A moment merely, out of the incomprehensible
immensity that is time; all of them decades dead,
save the baby, who is stooped now with age, where I

stand again, by the font; it is still that moment, they are
all there, attendant, as they were, and will be. Point
vierge. The spirit still moving over the waters.

*

I have sought a living poetry, written out of spirit
in the on-going love-affair between self and world,
to yield a deepening understanding and a widening

tenderness, that will save us from the hell of remorseless
logic, from transhumanism and artificial intelligence;
a poetry of verve and muscle, with insinuating music, no

versification for corners of the comics page; a poetry
of soul's integrity and venture. I would have words
of prophecy, holding the door ajar between past and now,

now and future, words to touch the heart of star
and starfish, of ancient lands where the people, in our time,
have been marshalled into darkness. The big book tells

how the Lord called Samuel the third time; he arose and went
to Eli and said, *Here I am, you called me*. And Eli knew it was
the Lord who called, and Eli said to Samuel: *Go, lie down;*

*if you hear the call again you will say: Speak, Lord, your servant
is listening*. I seek a garnering of words that touch beyond
the trite, towards transcendence, words laboured for and gifted,

so now I try for silence and sitting still, attendant on the spirit,
I question what I have come to, why so much time has been
allotted to me. I have attempted to play a plausible music,

beyond processes of was, and is, and will-be. Someday
there will be the final lines, last words will have been set down,
completed, and incomplete. Poems, like sycamore seeds, will be

free to wander in whatever breeze will take them, carrying
their burdens. I will have prayed: Spare me Lord for my days
burn off like dew, place, oh Christ, your angels as a fence about me.

*

The river was beautiful, dark water running smoothly before the rocks, silver-white and golden-ochre as it broke; below the rocks the pool, calm as if in world-satisfaction, promise in its depths.

Father fishing; absorbed in the world.

When he had the trout up on the bank, the sorrow began within me; that innocent lithe body, its gold-brown colouring, spots on its skin like miniature haloes; eye wide, unmoving, lips hard, mouth gasping.

Father put his thumb inside, forced back the head and I heard bones snapping. I almost wept; but this was my father fishing, who was spring and flow for me; he was absorbed, then, in the world but I felt something in creation's plan move towards disorder.

When the quintet stepped out onto the stage, I was sad, too; they were elderly, white-haired, fumbly, the door banged back behind them as they foostered towards the chairs, while I became aware of the hard bench under me.

Three old gentlemen; one old woman, a younger one at the piano.

They sat, ordering themselves to a settling of instruments, bows and strings, the piano stool, the tautness of the instruments like the stiffness of the flesh.

I was dismayed. Schubert: *Die Forelle*. Then

they began. Within moments, it was father again, absorbed in the world; there was an early summer breeze, the sun shone;

stream-water sparkled, fitting itself wholly into itself; earth
a joy, azure the unattainable sky; piano runs and playfulness,
strings like lithe bodies in fluid mastery.

When I opened my eyes I saw them, the elders, flux and
energy of their bodies absorbed from one another, moving
like reed-beds, like water-lilies and it was love, it was the
spirit breathing again through Genesis, as if the seniors were
extracting order and not imposing it; disparate they were,
shifting in their own breezes, yet shifting as one, their parts
moving, the whole refigured, segment and whole resolving.

I found myself, afterwards, exhausted, laid out on the green
fields of the world, hurt, and never so alive.

*

There was a storm, withering through the trees.
I was safe in the drawing-room. I had been
tinkering a little on the piano, had played
poorly. Frustrated again, I took up the poem;

waited. There was no stir. I must have dozed,
for it was surely dream that came to me. There were
three, like the staid and fetching angels who appeared
out of the desert before the tent of Abraham.

We sat, for a time and out of time; they asked,
without speaking. *I believe*, I answered, also
without speaking: *I believe I had said yes; I certify to this:
that God is true*. They said they had come to ring

the bells of evidence. I pleaded – no: I had not yet
credited the poem I was to write. Silence again.

I heard a small bell tinkling, like the bells of
Elevation. I whispered to them again – *No, I have not*

been proved worthy; and what, I asked, *what*
of the lover, Crucified? So: silence a while, for a time
and out of time. Till they seemed to fade, like dew
from leaves of the thorn-bush. I thought

I heard a bell toll somewhere in the distance.
I woke; the Angelus bell was sounding from
the monastery. There were three guttering candles
with wax starting to spill over on the piano lid.

*

I have turned a corner and find that I am old,
the language of my body is stuttering and slow;
age, like a mist,
has come upon me by surprise;

I have turned a corner and find that I am one
of a diminished generation, challenging old dogma –
but who have held firm
to the goal, the Omega, the Christ.

Today I watched an old, slowed ram, black-face,
wool shabby and tacked with clay, taking his ease
in the wet wild meadow
and gazing at his ewes from a distance; he was feeding

on bitter windfall apples in the sweetest aftergrass, a ram
not remorseful for his vanities, nor for the wicked
hard-bone spirals
of his horns. Now I find that the body,

in its mellow shrivelling, is nothing beautiful;
night-time, the eyes are more often open
on the slow-waltz
movements of star and planet. Night-time I hold

it is not necessary to kneel in judgement on the self,
to the Christ desire alone will be eloquent.
Now I sit, content,
on the canal-bank bench, watching the swans

worry at their feathers, white down gathering in beautiful
disorder, where I can honour the elderly-gentleman
elegance on the water,
the handsome dowager waddling across the grass.

LIKE THE DEWFALL

Amen of the Consummation

I stood, smitten and tongue-tied, and held the latch lest it slam
the thick paint-blistered door
between the dim-lit kitchen and the free yard outside
where green slime trailed down

the side of the water-butt. Maggie, too old, still young,
was bent double with arthritis;
she ushered me, kindly, in. The kitchen was time and place
of poverty and unwitting graciousness,

odour of age, of damp, of stone floors; you, too, oh Christ,
my Christ, were there, becurled and
ineffective, boasting, centre-chest, a heart on fire: presiding
over a damp-turf smoke-chocked fire.

Maggie, under her burden of skirts and woollens, sent me
down to the lower room to greet
her whine-voiced mother; in that cavern-dark space there was a reek
of blankets, urine, counterpanes,

the ancient woman dim and frightening, almost animal
in her stare and breathing;
I, child I, did not understand; it was an ending, slow and ugly,
an untriumphant eking-away of living;

she muttered something spittly at me, I nodded, turned, and
when I came back, Maggie
had wrapped the eggs in pages of "Ireland's Own". At last, to hear
the click of the latch behind me

was relief beyond relief. But your words echo still within me:
"blessed are you poor", and "come to me,
ye burdened". Now it is you, Oh Christ, my Christ, are begging,
you who are dying for my love.

*

At the bedrock of the cross I stand appalled;
at times I see you, Christ, barefoot by the lake,

praying; crowds crush forward, you – who have been
watching out over the water – turn to them,

heroic and alone. You have come upon me,
over decades, entering my heart, stealthily,

like the dewfall. Slaughters, disasters, assaults
burst in on our TV; the authorities,

upright folk, wring the usual words, presenting
vinegar. Nevertheless: *Haec nox est*, we will sing,

lest we forget. My words, of praise and pleading
– astonished still by your fierce, unmeasured love,

offered against despair and nothingness – fall
like stones, like teardrops, beneath your hurting feet.

*

A storm was crowding in off the Atlantic,
bringing darkness, rain
and sudden squalls; I sheltered in Bunnacurry church,
reading Isaiah: *"many were appalled at him;*

like one from whom the people hide their faces, he was
despised, and we held him
in low esteem". I looked up at the crucifix
over the altar; it was of silver and bronze, artfully wrought.

An old man was shuffling around the stations,
faded brown jacket, baggy
corduroys, mouthing the words in a muffled whisper;
old islandman, I thought, old faith. The winds cried, rains

spattered the windows. I closed my eyes awhile, wearied,
till I felt a hand touch me
on the shoulder; a man, of uncertain age, but old,
stood over me; he wore a robe of rough material, dark-wood

brown, brown leather belt, a long beard of purest white, white
hair, somewhat unkempt, to his shoulders.
It was the eyes, a light and piercing blue, that burned through
into my soul. "You have stolen up on me," I said,

"like a revenant." He smiled, then turned his gaze
to the crucifix, shivered a little. I suspected drink…
"That is not how it was," he whispered, pointing;
"not stylized, no comfort, no repose; can one go so deep

into the abyss, unshuddering?" He stood above me; "Who
are you?" I asked him. "I was," he said,
"John, brother to James, the sons of Zebedee. Sons
of Thunder," and he laughed, quietly. "I laid," he said,

"my head against his breast and knew that strong heart
beating, heart of the cosmos,
of the earth and heavens, source where love and life
are rooted. By night they dragged him, tortured, mocked him,

and around noon they crucified him outside the city wall.
I watched the one who is
source and sustenance, goal of a living universe
suffer more than any human ever ought to know; he writhed

against the timber, I could count his bones, I could not
turn away; a ragged loin-cloth was heavy
with his blood. Oh my Yeshua!" he sighed,
"you took upon yourself all knowledge of human suffering."

He paused, he took my right hand in a fierce grip, I could feel
the bones, and drew away from him, quickly. "We
took him down, rested the broken body on Miriam's lap. I
laid my head against his bloodied chest and that strong heart

had ceased to beat. The sky had turned black, the clay
trembled; I was certain
our world had ended." He sighed and fell silent a while. "But
we met again! in dawnlight, by the lakeshore, on his journey

back from the tomb. One more time I leant against his breast, knew
the strong and eternal beating
of his heart." He smiled at me, sighed again: "I was tasked,"
he said, "to live, unlike the others; tasked with words, to tell

of love, forgiveness, of the thrust of all creation's growth
towards that great heart."
"How," I asked him then, "how can I sing the Lord's song
in a dead land?" (Those piercing eyes!) "Trust," he said, "your voice,

your words. He is word. Speak him." I lowered my head,
closed my eyes, a moment, merely. Shaken.
When I looked up he was gone. There was only the old man
of the stations, lighting candles before the shrine of Mary.

*

In the nuns' garden the sisters stand apart, shy birds
on the shore of a pounding sea. I am awed
by the tongue's fidelity to silence, by the will's

self-confining strength in a bare cell. I had thought of them
as dead before they are dead. In the ordered graveyard
small iron crosses stand in their neat rows, names in faith,

dates of birth and death; over them all the delicate,
persistent blossoms of the saxifrage. I saw, in fissures
of sunlight, blue-glossed ravens exulting on the air;

there were scents of oleander, of thyme, of extravagant
heathers; I looked for the stillness of the high, white lily.
Beyond the walls, each day brings us reading in the papers

of yesterday's death routines. *Ein jeder Engel*, I remembered,
ist schrecklich; and do the angels fly, I wondered, late and late,
across the black night sky, to roost? The big book tells

that even the unproductive sand, the marram, the sand-eel,
will flush, after all, into the joy of the festive song of songs
across all the unthinkable, all-sainted, infinite demesnes of God.

*

Day dying in the outer suburbs; a quiet,
settling. Unfussed, relishing – alongside

the woman he loves – boxty potato pancakes
with parsley butter melting over; shrimp,

in garlic and lemon, sizzling on the skillet;
a pinot grigio, that honeysuckle flavour…

Then stands outside in the warm dusk, faint
sounds of distant traffic, scarcely a zephyr-breath

touching the high ash-trees; the soft shudder
of a boiler coming to life. Earlier he had walked

where mallard and water-hen had been busy
about their mating rituals, their rushes and flurries

across the waters of the canal, stirred by original
freshness and urgency. He inhaled, luxuriously; knew

that the people whom he loved were here, revelling,
everywhere around, and waiting. Night closing in;

soon, raspberry and rhubarb crumble, with a small
dollop of cream; a film, perhaps, on the TV;

anticipating always the savoury heaviness of sleep.
Brittle-hipped, a little arthritic and taut of hearing,

climbing contentedly, but cautiously, upstairs.
Amen, he says, Amen; oh Christ, my Christ, Amen

ACKNOWLEDGMENTS

Reading Ireland: USA, *Agenda* (UK), *Ireland of the Welcomes*, *Irish Pages*, *The Poetry Ireland Review*, *The Irish Times*, *The Stinging Fly*, *Agenda* (UK), *Temenos Academy Review* (UK), *The Tablet* (UK), *PN Review* (UK), *Poem* (UK), *Long Poem Magazine* (UK), *Stride Magazine* (UK), *Raceme* (UK), *Image Journal* (USA), *Salamander* (USA}, *Presence* (USA), *Indian Poetry Journal*, *Poetry International.*

A version of 'Death Lullaby' appeared in the anthology *Fermata,* ed. Eva Bourke and Vincent Woods; 'Colmán on Lindisfarne' was published in the book *The Hippocrates Book of the Heart,* ed. Wendy French, Michael Hulse, Donald Singer; 'Found in the Margins: 6th Century' was published under a different title in *Reading the Future: 250 Years of Hodges Figgis* and broadcast on RTÉ Radio One, *Sunday Miscellany.*

3 poems from the 'Send Word' sequence were published in *Triptychs* by Guillemot Press, UK, in 2017; the poem 'By-The-Wind Sailor' was published in *Long Poem Magazine*, and in a French translation by Jacques Rancourt in *Agenda.*

The poem 'Quartet for the End of Time' was originally published in a festschrift for Fr Brendan McConvery C.Ss.R.: *The Cultural Reception of the Bible* (Four Courts Press 2018).

Note: 'Jack Gilbert says, Nevertheless': cf. Jack Gilbert, 'A Stubborn Ode', *The Great Fires* (Knopf 1994).

Note: 'Like The Dewfall' – The French composer Olivier Messiaen (1908-1992) wrote a suite of seven pieces for two pianos, composed and performed in 1943 during the Nazi Occupation of Paris. He called the suite 'Visions de l'Amen', 'Visions of the Amen'; Messiaen describes the music as seven visions reflecting the lives of those who say 'Amen', accepting the details of their existence with gratitude. I owe a debt of gratitude to the book *Visions of Amen*, by Stephen Schloesser, Professor of history at Loyola University, Chicago. The book is published by Wm. B. Eedermans Publishing Co., Michigan, 2014.

The poem sequence 'Like the Dewfall' was published by Guillemot Press, UK, in December 2019 in a special edition limited to 250 copies, with artwork by Tony Martin. With gratitude to Luke Thompson, editor, and to Tony Martin.